Transforming Teaching & Learning

Developing 'Critical Skills' for living and working in the 21st century

Colin Weatherley
with Bruce Bonney
John Kerr & Jo Morrison

Published by Network Educational Press Ltd
PO Box 635
Stafford
ST16 1BF

First published 2003
© Colin Weatherley, Bruce Bonney, John Kerr & Jo Morrison 2003

ISBN 1 85539 080 9

Series Editor: Professor Tim Brighouse
Project Manager: Anne Oppenheimer
Design & layout: Neil Hawkins, NEP
Illustrations: Kerry Ingham

Printed in Great Britain by
MPG Books Ltd, Bodmin, Cornwall

Foreword

A teacher's task is much more ambitious than it used to be and demands a focus on the subtleties of teaching and learning and on the emerging knowledge of school improvement.

This is what this series is about.

Teaching can be a very lonely activity. The time-honoured practice of a single teacher working alone in the classroom is still the norm; yet to operate alone is, in the end, to become isolated and impoverished. This series addresses two issues – the need to focus on practical and useful ideas connected with teaching and learning and the wish thereby to provide some sort of an antidote to the loneliness of the long-distance teacher who is daily berated by an anxious society.

Teachers flourish best when, in key stage teams or departments (or more rarely whole schools), their talk is predominantly about teaching and learning and where, unconnected with appraisal, they are privileged to observe each other teach; to plan and review their work together; and to practise the habit of learning from each other new teaching techniques. But how does this state of affairs arise? Is it to do with the way staffrooms are physically organized so that the walls bear testimony to interesting articles and in the corner there is a dedicated computer tuned to 'conferences' about SEN, school improvement, the teaching of English etc., and whether, in consequence, the teacher leaning over the shoulder of the enthusiastic IT colleague sees the promise of interesting practice elsewhere? Has the primary school cracked it when it organizes successive staff meetings in different classrooms and invites the 'host' teacher to start the meeting with a 15 minute exposition of their classroom organization and management? Or is it the same staff sharing, on a rota basis, a slot on successive staff meeting agendas when each in turn reviews a new book they have used with their class? And what of the whole-school which now uses 'active' and 'passive' concerts of carefully chosen music as part of their accelerated learning techniques?

It is of course well understood that even excellent teachers feel threatened when first they are observed. Hence the epidemic of trauma associated with OFSTED. The constant observation of the teacher in training seems like that of the learner driver. Once you have passed your test and can drive unaccompanied, you do. You often make lots of mistakes and sometimes get into bad habits. Woe betide, however, the back seat driver who tells you so. In the same way, the new teacher quickly loses the habit of observing others and being observed. So how do we get a confident, mutual observation debate going? One school I know found a simple and therefore brilliant solution. The Head of the History Department asked that a young colleague plan lessons for her – the Head of Department – to teach. This lesson she then taught, and was observed by the young colleague. There was subsequent discussion, in which the young teacher asked,

> "Why did you divert the question and answer session I had planned?"

and was answered by,

> "Because I could see that I needed to arrest the attention of the group by the window with some 'hands-on' role play, etc."

This lasted an hour and led to a once-a-term repeat discussion which, in the end, was adopted by the whole-school. The whole-school subsequently changed the pattern of its meetings to consolidate extended debate about teaching and learning. The two teachers claimed that, because one planned and the other taught, both were implicated but neither alone was responsible or felt 'got at'.

So there are practices which are both practical and more likely to make teaching a rewarding and successful activity. They can, as it were, increase the likelihood of a teacher surprising the pupils into understanding or doing something they did not think they could do rather than simply entertaining them or worse still occupying them. There are ways of helping teachers judge the best method of getting pupil expectation just ahead of self-esteem.

This series focuses on straightforward interventions which individual schools and teachers use to make life more rewarding for themselves and those they teach. Teachers deserve nothing less, for they are the architects of tomorrow's society, and society's ambition for what they achieve increases as each year passes.

Professor Tim Brighouse

Notes on the Main Contributors

Colin Weatherley is a former secondary headteacher in West Lothian and Edinburgh. In 1998 he discovered the Critical Skills Programme in an American INSET video series. Network Educational Press were so impressed with the videos and other CSP materials that they negotiated the exclusive rights to promote CSP in the UK and asked Colin to take on the role of UK Critical Skills Manager.

Bruce Bonney is a former middle school teacher in New York State. He trained in CSP in 1990, and after several years of teaching with the model joined the Critical Skills Program headquarters staff. He is now President of Leading EDGE LLC, which organises all CSP training in New York State. Since early 2000 he has also worked closely with Network Educational Press to develop UK CSP training.

John Kerr is head of the history department at Balerno Community High School, Edinburgh, and a senior examiner with the Scottish Qualifications Authority. He was one of the first UK teachers to undertake CSP training in February 2000 and has recently become an accredited CSP trainer.

Jo Morrison was the first UK teacher to become an accredited CSP trainer. She works with 15- to 16-year-old underachieving and disaffected students at Tresham Institute, Kettering. CSP has given a solid framework to her work and has revitalised not only Jo but also her students.

Contents

Section One: Introduction

1. A Brief History of the Critical Skills Programme in the UK

Colin Weatherley

On Boxing Day 1998 a mysterious package thumped through my letterbox. It was from Bruce Bonney, President of Leading EDGE LLC, New York State. Despite being unsolicited – and also slightly late – it was to prove one of the most interesting and challenging Christmas presents I have ever received! Inside the package was a letter from Bruce telling me that he had been told of my interest in the Critical Skills Programme and that he was enclosing two copies of the Level 1 Coaching Manual, together with samples of other CSP materials.

When I finally made time to read them I realised that they were by some way the most impressive collection of teaching and learning materials that I had ever seen. They epitomised in practical and comprehensive detail the application of all the key theoretical principles of learning that I had been reading about and attempting to apply over the previous decade. Little did I realise then, however, just what an impact they were to have on my life.

In his letter Bruce had recommended me to contact Pete Fox, an outstanding New York State English teacher and one of his top CSP trainers, who was due to visit London in the Spring of 1999. This I did, and with the enthusiastic support of Ian Glen, then Curriculum Manager for the City of Edinburgh Education Department, I persuaded Pete and his wife, Jane, to come to Edinburgh to lead what turned out to be an outstandingly successful seminar, in April 1999.*

*For further details of this seminal occasion see the summary of Pete's vignette on page 15 and John Kerr's vignette (page 87).

I also sent a copy of the Coaching Manual to Chris Dickinson at Network Educational Press. Some weeks later Chris phoned to say that he had finally found time to read it. His clear excitement was such that I thought he was in danger of coming through the phone!

We both agreed that the promotion of CSP had the potential to become one of the most significant events in recent UK educational history. But at that stage we were quite uncertain how – or even whether – this could be done, given the considerable extra expense of bringing qualified CSP trainers across the Atlantic, and the severe limitations on their availability, given that almost all of them are themselves full-time teachers.*

* The motto of CSP is: 'Teachers teaching teachers.'

Fortunately, following that initial seminar I had made contact with Craig Campbell of CBI Scotland,* who informed me that the CBI was convinced that the UK education system was not preparing young people for the world of life and work effectively enough.* Craig immediately realised the significance of CSP and was able to secure a generous grant from the Clydesdale Bank. With continuing support and commitment from Edinburgh Council via Ian Glen, we were then able to finance the cost of bringing over a group of Critical Skills Master Teacher/Trainers to run Level 1 training in Edinburgh in February 2000.

* Craig Campbell is now Director of Community Banking with the Bank of Scotland.

* This precisely echoes the conclusions of the 1981 Carnegie Commission report which led to the setting up of CSP (see page 32).

* Forrest Howie, John Kerr and Brian Speedie were among this initial cohort of trainees. Their vignettes clearly convey the sense of excitement that Pete, Jane, Bruce and Jack generated. (See Section 3, Vignettes 2, 5 and 7.)

The group consisted of Pete and Jane Fox, Bruce Bonney and Bruce's colleague Jack Drury. The impact that they made on some 50 teachers from Edinburgh and West Lothian* was quite dramatic. It was clear that these teachers shared our enthusiasm for 'Critical Skills'.

It was at that point that Chris Dickinson took the decision that, whatever the organisational and financial difficulties, this was an opportunity that had to be fully grasped. The Critical Skills Programme clearly had the potential to make a major, beneficial impact on the UK educational scene. Therefore Network Educational Press would invest whatever was necessary to ensure that this potential was achieved as speedily and effectively as possible.

Events so far have fully justified our faith in 'Critical Skills'. Some 50 teachers completed Level 1 training in 2000, but by the end of 2002 this number will have risen to well over 600. And the overwhelming response to the training has been one of great enthusiasm, typified by the following selection of comments from Scottish teachers who completed some of the earlier rounds of training, in 1991:

> 'This is by far the most useful course I have ever attended... I have great expectations and hope to continue as a Critical Skills practitioner.' (Catherine Donaldson, Head of Home Economics, Midlothian)
>
> 'This course has been an inspiration. All the trainers obviously speak with a very high level of experience and commitment. More please!' (Isabel Marshall, Primary Teacher, Midlothian)
>
> 'This was a fantastic course! It was very practical, 'hands on' and worthwhile. I can't wait to get back to school and try some more! ... Thank you!' (Caroline Findlay, Primary School Teacher, Midlothian)
>
> 'CSP was the only in-service course I've ever been on that I never wanted to stop!' (Sue Stephen, Nursery School Teacher, Midlothian)
>
> 'The whole process has been inspirational. It is stimulating and gives the opportunity to motivate all pupils to develop essential life skills... I feel I have grown as an individual and look forward to implementing the programme fully in school.' (Joan Herald, Assistant Headteacher, Newton Mearns)
>
> 'A first-class course. There was so much learning at a theoretical and a practical level that was so skilfully blended to make a complete learning experience that it's hard to believe that it happened in little more than 36 hours!' (Lesley Robertson, Primary Adviser, Clackmannanshire)
>
> 'A great experience... I see so many avenues ahead to benefit my teaching and the pupils' learning – as well as helping me to 'Lead a Learning School' more effectively' (Alison Fox, Primary School Headteacher, West Lothian)

CSP has now spread into all parts of the UK and demand is beginning to significantly outstrip supply. We are therefore working hard to identify and train our own corps of

UK-based trainers who will enable us to begin to meet more of this burgeoning demand, and at times that are more convenient to UK schools.

The word is out! 'Critical Skills' is a comprehensive and immensely powerful teaching programme that enables teachers and school managers to tackle all the key current issues of UK education in a uniquely effective way. As Midlothian primary teacher Gillian Grant observed:

'And the best thing – it works!'

* **Leading the Learning School** (Network Educational Press 2000)

When Network Educational Press asked me to write a book on school leadership* I thought that I would use CSP as one of several examples of learning and teaching programmes that could provide the focus for development planning in a 'learning school'. But as I learned more about the programme and saw its impact on teachers and schools, I came to realise that CSP was different from all the other programmes I had encountered. It was both more practical and more comprehensive. As NEP's Managing Director, Jim Houghton, commented when he first saw the materials:

'These are the first training materials I have seen that are more than just a set of good ideas for applying modern research on learning in the classroom. They represent a comprehensive, very practical and highly impressive training package which clearly has the potential to revolutionise classroom practice as well as school management.'

Or as Chris Dickinson characteristically put it:

'The difference between CSP and other learning and teaching programmes is a bit like the difference between a training course for chefs and a set of recipe books. Recipe books are full of good ideas for individual dishes and may also give you some ideas for combining them, but to develop the complete range of skills to become a professional chef you need to go through the training course.'

So, far from being a side reference as I had originally thought, CSP came to form the core of *Leading the Learning School*. Very soon people who had read that book and/or taken part in CSP training began to ask if we could produce a second book devoted entirely to CSP; one that could form a reference for those wishing to use CSP in their classrooms and schools. This is our response to that request.

Our aim in writing this book has been fourfold:

1. **To provide basic information about the Critical Skills Programme** – how it developed; its underpinning theory; and how the materials and methods are used to translate that theory into such effective practice.

2. **To provide examples of 'real life' experiences with CSP** – in primary, secondary and further education classrooms; at whole-school and education authority levels; and on both sides of the Atlantic.

3. **To show how CSP can be used to transform whole schools as well as individual classrooms** – by creating a collaborative culture throughout the school and promoting effective staff development and development planning.

4. **To show how CSP can be used to address major national educational objectives** – how it uses challenging problem-solving activities, individual target-setting and formative assessment to raise expectations; motivate and engage; and promote the development of essential knowledge, key skills and fundamental attitudes.

2. A Summary of the Book
John Kerr and Colin Weatherley

The book contains five sections, including this introduction. It is copiously cross–referenced by means of margin notes throughout. This is for two reasons:

➡ first, to illustrate how the general description of the model and its underpinning theory (Section 2) links to the detailed descriptions of the model in action in a wide variety of educational situations (Sections 3 to 5).

➡ second, to enable readers to 'dip in' to the book for reference purposes rather than having to read from cover to cover to make sense of the descriptions.

Section 2: The Critical Skills Programme: The 'Big Picture'

This section provides an overview of the programme. After a brief description of the genesis of CSP, John Kerr takes us step-by-step through the Critical Skills Programme Experiential Cycle, describing how the four *broad ideas* which underpin CSP are implemented so effectively in the various phases of the cycle. John also describes some of the most important of the many highly effective CSP *tools*. For clarity, first references to these tools in Section 2, and in each of the vignettes in Section 3, are highlighted in italics.

Section 3: The Critical Skills Programme in Action

This section presents ten vignettes by CSP practitioners:

Vignette 1: The Gilboa-Conesville Experience

– is by **Pete Fox**, English teacher extraordinary at Gilboa-Conesville Central School in upstate New York. As already noted (page 11), Pete and his wife Jane provided the initial UK 'CSP Experience' in the form of a one-day seminar in Edinburgh in April 1999. This was a remarkable occasion in that Pete and Jane ran a highly experiential and very successful workshop for 84 people, as vividly described by John Kerr in Vignette No. 5 (page 87). It was the enthusiastic response to this initial CSP experience that provided the impetus to organise the first round of Level 1 CSP training in February 2000, as described in 'A Brief History of CSP in the UK' (page 11).

Pete describes how Gilboa-Conesville had, by 1992, become an archetypal 'failing school' – bottom of the state examination league tables and with high levels of indiscipline and vandalism. Despite his own personal teaching successes he had finally decided to look for a career outwith teaching. At the last minute he was persuaded by his School Principal, Matt Murray, to attend a week-long Level 1 CSP training institute in the summer vacation.

The institute was run by Bruce Bonney (see 'A Brief History' (page 11) and Section 4), and the experiential nature of the activities meant that the first morning was a big turnoff for Pete, whose own style of teaching at that time he describes as the 'Grand Lecturer'. By lunchtime he had announced his intention to leave but, fortunately for Gilboa – and UK education – Bruce managed to persuade him to stay for the afternoon. And the rest, as they say, is history!

Pete returned to Gilboa determined to try out this new model of teaching which, although not a natural style for him, 'was the me I needed to become ... to meet the needs of my students'. Matt Murray and the school superintendent, Joe Beck, were very supportive and 'created a safe environment in which teachers were encouraged to take risks'. Within weeks Pete's students were spreading the message round the school that this was a teaching approach that energised them and enabled them to achieve high standards of knowledge, skills and commitment to life; and many of Pete's colleagues were clamouring to take the training themselves.

The main message of Pete's vignette is that application of the CSP model in a school can lead to dramatic improvements; but this will only happen if the school's senior management team are prepared to engage with the model and to encourage their teachers to take the kind of risks that we all must take if we are to learn at a deep level. As Bruce Bonney himself says: 'Learning always occurs at the edge of our comfort zone.'

Vignette 2: A Primary Class Teacher's Experience

– is by **Forrest Howie**, Senior Teacher at Sciennes Primary School, Edinburgh. Like many CSP teachers, Forrest started his Level 1 training with a healthy degree of scepticism, born of several unsatisfactory previous in-service experiences. But by the end of the training, and more particularly after two years of putting the CSP model into practice, he felt 'enthused, empowered and revitalised' – another common experience.

Forrest describes how, with three very different Year 7 classes, there were long periods of time when every child in the class was 'on task' – something which he had not encountered before and which he describes as 'brilliant... This empowered the children – and it definitely empowered me!'

He makes the important point that CSP represents a 'development not a revolution' and that it still provides plenty of opportunity for 'good old-fashioned teaching'. The *scenario challenge* that he designed required his pupils to work collaboratively as teams of 'journalists' to prepare articles for a daily newspaper. But before they tackled the team part of the challenge Forrest used some 'good old-fashioned teaching' to help them learn how to write a newspaper report.

Forrest highlights two further issues. First, that the CSP model allowed him to devote much more time to *formative assessment*, using self- and peer- as well as teacher-assessment. He makes the important point that this was made more powerful by the way in which pupils discussed the *performance criteria* before they started the challenge – in the process of *chunking the challenge* – so that they were clear about what they were expected to do.

As Forrest observes: 'Assessment through ... CSP ... became manageable, useful, clear and – dare I say it – fun!' But this heightened role for formative assessment did not stop with the pupils. Importantly, he also received feedback and reflected upon his own performance – a classic example of the way in which the model can apply as much to teachers as to their pupils.

Finally, Forrest relates how his pupils 'spread the word' to their parents, not least by the fact that many of them would take challenge work home to complete so as not to let their group down. Again, this is a common example of the power of the model in generating motivation and helping to integrate homework into pupils' general class-work in a meaningful way.

Vignette 3: Re-visioning Revision: An English Teacher's Experience

– is by **Audrey Gibson**, Assistant Head of the English department in Cumnock Academy, Ayrshire. Audrey's description of how CSP changed her practice reinforces many key principles of CSP. Her students solved a real problem, and in so doing took ownership of their work, while the inspiration for the challenge that sparked the process and product was directly linked to Audrey's own experiences in Level 1 CSP training.

Audrey's account starts in territory familiar to many teachers. Despite having been taught how to tackle the Standard Grade Close Reading examination, her pupils had failed to apply this information and so had done poorly in their 'prelim.' examination. How often have we had this experience, where skills or content taught in the lesson are abandoned by pupils under some degree of pressure? Are pupils wilfully ignoring teachers' advice, or is there disconnection between theory and practice? In fact, just because a skill or content is taught, is that reason enough for some pupils to reject it? In this example of CSP in practice, the programme not only provided motivation and engagement but also the bridge between learning and doing.

It was when considering this gap between lesson content and her pupils' use of that work that Audrey remembered a key challenge in Level 1 training – the 'Tower of Power Scenario Challenge'. Her account of understanding S.T.O.P. (Standard Teachers Operating Procedure), and its crucial importance to working collaboratively and purposefully – and then abandoning it under pressure! – will strike chords of familiarity with most of us who have been there.

The *challenge* which Audrey designed asked her pupils to prepare a guidebook to help other pupils prepare for the Close Reading exam. Having designed the challenge, Audrey describes how she established a *learning community* through the application of standard CSP tools. In so doing she explores the implications for discipline; ownership; and her pupils' accountability for their actions and decisions.

Audrey stresses the need for concrete *content, form* and *rule criteria*; and as the pupils engaged with the challenge Audrey recounts how they became involved in the process and almost automatically adopted CSP principles and tools to their advantage – even refining their work as they went through the stages of the challenge. Audrey also discovered one of the hardest lessons for teachers – the need to stand back and leave the pupils to engage productively with the task.

At the end of the challenge the pupils had produced work of value to themselves and others. Their self-esteem was enhanced and the content and skills which had previously been taught but then ignored were now well rooted. Most important, it was *their* work, *their* pride and *their* success.

Vignette 4: A Special Needs Teacher's Experience

– is by **Heather Swinson**, a Learning Support Teacher at St David's High School, Dalkeith, Midlothian. Her account focuses on work with a group of disaffected pupils whose self-esteem was often low and whose enthusiasm for learning had waned.

The first part of her account deals with her first contact with CSP, and may well strike chords with others. Expecting a standard style of in-service provision, Heather soon discovered what is meant by *experiential learning*. She was part of a new *learning community*, coming to terms with new ideas, new challenges and new expectations. In fact, very much the experience of many pupils in schools attending a new class! However, Heather makes the important point that within this maelstrom of new experiences she was confronted with many powerful educational theories. This reminds us that CSP is not out on a limb; rather, it is based on good practice and sound educational principles.

The second part of Heather's article deals with her attemps to use CSP methods back in school. Her account reads as a 'master class' in establishing a learning community with a *Full Value Contract*, employing various tools including *brainstorming* and agreements over *quality audience* and *quality discussion*. Heather also makes clear that while the challenge she designed was a real life challenge, she was also aware that the process should require pupils to use or acquire 'critical skills' and 'fundamental dispositions' (attitudes) that were not always evident in their methods of working!

The journey towards the achievement of the challenge is a fascinating tale of motivation and changing attitudes, but also of important lessons being learned by Heather as she reflected on her role within the learning community. Overall, she identifies the major successes of CSP as developing self-esteem and significantly improving the behaviour of her pupils – as witnessed and commented upon by an HM Inspector! Her accounts of 'schoolopoly' in operation vividly illustrate the motivation that comes from CSP in the classroom.

Finally, Heather perceptively describes the change in attitude that came over her group. When faced with difficulties, CSP methods and tools enabled them to change one-time 'stumbling stones' into 'stepping stones'.

Vignette 5: 'Enhancing Classroom Learning': A Head of Department's Experience

– is by **John Kerr**, Head of History at Balerno Community High School, Edinburgh. At first John charts his initial response to CSP – an experience provided at Pete Fox's first UK seminar (see page 11). In many ways this reflects the experiences recounted by Pete himself (see page 66), that is initial wariness and a degree of cynicism changing into a realisation that here was something of real practical value which cut through the pragmatic thick skin of long-term teachers. Was it that the presentation of Pete Fox lit a fire, rekindled a spark – or did it just provide the necessary impetus to stand back from the daily hurly-burly and think about the how and the why of what is happening in our classrooms?

Some criticisms of CSP revolve around time and content. Is there enough time and will teachers have time to cover a syllabus? John shows that with imagination and the use of structured *challenges*, content can be 'delivered' in effective ways to all high-school year groups, along with the desired learning outcomes implicit and explicit in the various national guidelines and syllabuses. There is also a reminder that CSP is particularly apposite to the burgeoning pressures of the citizenship agenda.

The article reminds all practitioners that they will not invent perfection every time and the encouragement to *reflect and review* work applies just as much to teachers and coaches as it does to pupils. CSP is an experiential model for everyone.

The spin-off benefits of CSP – particularly in improving discipline – are highlighted, and consideration is given to questions of *assessment*.

The article then raises more political questions. In John's experience of introducing CSP to new teachers he is struck by the appropriateness of the methodology and also the great enthusiasm of the teachers; and yet in some areas school managers and local authority education officers are less enthusiastic. To paraphrase the old review of a Bruce Springsteen performance, having experienced CSP training John has seen a vision of the future of education – and it works!

| Vignette 6: A Secondary Whole-School Perspective |

– is by **Linda Marshall**, Assistant Headteacher at Central Lancaster High School, with a background in teaching religious education and an abiding interest in effective teaching methodology. She has a particular responsibility in her school for the development of teaching and learning.

With an awareness of various learning theories Linda describes how she approached CSP with an open mind; unsure what she would discover, or how the new programme would link with present practice and the demands put upon her by national guidelines and government inspectors. However, in her own words, CSP provided the 'picture on the lid of the jigsaw', combining learning theory and good teaching practice into a practical and encompassing package of direct use and of inspirational quality. Linda goes on to describe how she was struck during her Level 1 training, not only by the possibilities of CSP application in a classroom but also how it could be applied to a whole-school with transforming possibilities.

As a person already involved in supported self study and in writing study guides for pupils, the writing of the *challenges* did not pose a great problem to Linda; but she relates how the *debriefing* stage led on to a time of reflection and then review of pupil and teacher material, thereby illustrating the *experiential cycle* model of challenge, debrief and progression onto the next cycle.

Linda tells of the ups and downs of using CSP in her school, listing positive achievements but also the problems encountered. Most helpfully and revealingly, Linda also offers some possible solutions, illustrating that a teacher using CSP should always be open to the possibility of failure at times and the need to review and try a new route.

Linda then goes on to outline future plans in her school and makes the point that in this educational world of frequent new initiatives, teachers will have to be convinced of the worth of CSP before they embark on a whole-school programme. It will not happen overnight. Some teachers within the school must lead the way, both as practitioners in their classroom – where hopefully pupils will carry the torch – but also as providers of training for school in-services. As Linda tellingly states, it is much easier to set up a *collaborative learning community* if you also work in one!

| Vignette 7: Using the CSP Model in Curriculum Development |

– is by **Brian Speedie**, Senior Teacher at Bruntsfield Primary School, Edinburgh. At the time of their Level 1 training Brian and Forrest Howie were colleagues at Bruntsfield. Brian describes how he, like Forrest, first of all used the CSP tools described in Section 2 to create a *collaborative climate* in his Year 7 classroom. This is always an essential first step but in Brian's case it was doubly so since, as he says: 'the children ... had many strengths but working together wasn't one of them'!

Having successfully transformed his classroom environment, Brian then turned his attention to the development of a whole-school approach to the Environmental Studies curriculum. Recognising that teamwork and the free flow of information between all members of staff were vital to the success of such a project, Brian realised that the same CSP tools which had been so effective with his pupils were likely to be equally effective with staff. Therefore he and Forrest used the CSP model to run a whole-school in-service day for their colleagues.

After a basic introduction to tools such as *brainstorming* and the *Full Value Contract* they moved on to use these tools to promote teamwork and a *collaborative culture* among the staff. This has proved to be of great benefit since, as Brian puts it: 'over the past few months staff have worked together extremely effectively to develop a long-term planning framework for Environmental Studies.'

Brian's experience is echoed by many other school managers who have similarly used the CSP model to promote effective collaboration among their staff. However, two further issues are worthy of note.

First, Brian's initiative would not have been nearly so effective without the support of his headteacher, Barbara Boyd, who not only encouraged Brian and Forrest to attend the initial training but also – in Pete Fox's words – 'created a safe environment in which teachers were encouraged to take risks'.

Second, as Brian himself notes, although his colleagues now have a certain facility with some of the CSP tools and a very positive attitude towards the programme as a whole, further CSP training for them in the near future is an absolute priority.

Vignette 8: Using the CSP Model with Staff and Pupils

– is by **Anne Callan**, Headteacher of Murrayfield Primary School in Blackburn, West Lothian. Anne's approach to implementation of CSP was almost exactly the opposite of Brian Speedie's, in that she first used it with her staff before trying it out with a difficult Year 7 class.

Anne and a fellow West Lothian headteacher, Alison Fox, went through Level 1 and Level 2 training together and have worked collaboratively since their Level 1 Part A training to develop methods of using the model at the whole-school level. Anne relates the story of their joint approach to the implementation of the McCrone Agreement on Scottish Teachers' Conditions of Service – and thereby hangs a considerable tale!

Some months ago Anne phoned Colin Weatherley to report that a senior member of West Lothian Directorate had visited her own and Alison Fox's schools and been much impressed. The visit had been arranged because the Directorate had become aware that these two headteachers had been able to gain the agreement of their staffs to the McCrone proposals with unusual speed and effectiveness. Clearly something special was going on in these two schools and they wanted to know what it was.

As Anne describes, 'CSP' was what was going on! By using CSP tools originally designed for pupils in classrooms, Anne and Alison had enabled their teachers to gain a good understanding of the McCrone proposals in a remarkably short time. And this in turn had led to the speedy resolution of any potential difficulties in implementation – a powerful example of the value of the model at all levels of management. It is well worth reading Anne's and Brian Speedie's vignettes in conjunction with Bruce Bonney's 'CSP in Your School: Greenhouse or Gobi? Advice for Senior Managers' (page 127) since they powerfully exemplify some of Bruce's general advice in action.

Following this success with her staff, Anne then used the model with a 'disaffected and unhappy' Year 7 class – again, with remarkably successful results. Indeed, the aforementioned phone call was occasioned by Anne's elation at the outcome of this, her first *challenge* to pupils. As Anne related it, at the end of the day two of the more disaffected boys had come up to her and said: 'Miss, you really made us work today, didn't you?' And they didn't seem to mind – in fact they had clearly revelled in the experience! As many other CSP teachers have found, if teachers put in the work to develop an effective *collaborative learning community* and design effective challenges, at the end of a typical CSP lesson the pupils are more tired than the teacher. Isn't that just how it should be?!

Vignette 9: Critical Signs and Clear Portents

– is by **Rick Lee**, a former drama teacher who is now Raising Achievement Co-ordinator with Barrow-in-Furness Community Learning Partnership (Education Action Zone). Rick brings the insights gained over many years of teaching drama to provide a vivid description of the experiences that he and his Action Zone colleagues went through in the first of Barrow's Level 1 training packages. Barrow EAZ was one of the first UK organisations to book a complete Level 1 training package, and Rick's description of the way in which the training experience produced a 'strong community of revitalised practitioners' is a powerful illustration of the benefits that such packages can bring.

As Bruce Bonney points out in 'Staying Alive with CSP' (page 123, 'Seek out friends and allies'): 'debriefing and reflecting on our CSP experience is crucial to our growth as a learner'. And this process is much more likely to happen when schools and authorities send groups of teachers who can themselves become, in Rick's words, 'a strong community,' able to support each other between training experiences through 'peer coaching' – a process of focused reflection and feedback that enables teachers to internalise the many sophisticated teaching skills that CSP provides.

Of course, there are always outstanding individual teachers who through personality and/or relevant experience are able to use such sophisticated skills effectively, almost regardless of their teaching environment. These are well exemplified by the vignette writers themselves. However, even these teachers will benefit much more from the peer support provided by the kind of strong community of 'learning teachers' described by Rick.

In this regard, it is worth noting that Barrow EAZ have now committed the major part of their staff development budget to CSP training packages for their teachers. These bring the added benefit of focused support from the trainers themselves who are able to visit novice practitioners in their classrooms and provide valuable – and extremely expert – feedback.

One other issue highlighted by Rick is the fact that CSP actually contains nothing new in terms of content. All the tools for the CSP classroom that are described in such effective action in Section 3 have been tried out somewhere at some time by someone (usually many people) and found to work. Indeed, that is a major strength of the programme.

But as Rick notes, the real power of CSP is the way in which 'lots of good practice has been synthesised into a holistic approach'. As Linda Marshall observes in Vignette 6: 'All the theories about pupil learning, teaching methodology, learning styles, assessment and pupil motivation could suddenly be "fitted" into a structure which made sense.' Or as Pete Fox puts it in his inimitable way: 'Old dogs can learn new tricks; and old tricks can still work for young dogs'!

> ## Vignette 10: The Box of Frogs:
> ### A Further Education Perspective

– is by **Jo Morrison**, who teaches 'disinterested and disaffected' teenagers at Tresham Institute of Further and Higher Education, Kettering, Northants. It is a dramatic account of the impact that CSP training and subsequent classroom experience had on a teacher who had all but given up hope of interesting her students in any worthwhile learning.

Starting with a vivid – but highly recognisable! – description of the characteristics of the individual members of her class, and the extremes of pessimism to which they had driven her, Jo goes on to describe the impact which the first part of her Level 1 CSP training had on her. She was particularly fortunate in being able to do this training in New York State, with two close colleagues of Bruce Bonney (see below). So, in addition to the training experience itself, Jo also had the opportunity to visit some 'CSP Schools', including Gilboa-Conesville Central School where Pete Fox taught.

As Jo relates: 'The school visits provided compelling evidence that the scheme worked. The kids were friendly, polite(!) and collaborative; and their standard of work refreshingly high... So I came back at the end of the October half term and ... told the students that I was unhappy; that the current situation wasn't working; and that I was going to try something different... Within two weeks, colleagues were asking me what was happening. How come the students were so different?'

Jo goes on to describe how she was able to use the CSP model so effectively. '...two things in particular created change in my classroom... the overt emphasis laid on the *skills* I want my students to exhibit ... (and) ... the range of *feedback* mechanisms, which held up a mirror to my students.' Jo, of course, is an exceptionally gifted teacher and so she was able to help her students cope successfully with the inevitable failure that followed their first few attempts to meet her 'challenges'. She insisted that they 'look into the mirror' (that is, review and reflect) by brainstorming the reasons for their failures. And 'without intervention from me, the students came up with things like: "We need to listen"... "We need to take on individual responsibility".'

By the end of the academic year Jo's students were 'a different bunch of kids. They were working together, trying really hard not to make the staff unhappy...' And she finishes with the following observation: 'I personally believe that CSP is **THE** way forward for education in the UK... It is broken, and we need to mend it. This is the repair kit.'

Section 4: Lessons from the USA

This section contains three articles by Bruce Bonney. All are based on the extensive experience Bruce has accumulated in working with the CSP model for over a decade – first as a front line teacher of 13–18 year olds; then as a member of the Critical Skills Program staff at Antioch New England Graduate School; and finally in setting up his own training organisation, Leading EDGE, LLC, to train teachers in New York State.

Bruce, of course, has played a crucial role in the introduction and development of CSP in the UK, as described in 'A Brief History of CSP in the UK' at the beginning of this section (page 11). In the first two articles he distils his extensive experience with the model to provide insightful and highly authoritative advice for newly trained CSP teachers and senior education managers respectively.

The dominant theme of **Article 1: Staying Alive with CSP: Advice for Newly Trained Critical Skills Teachers** is summed up in the following sentence:

'As I understand it, the CSP model is a coherent and effective framework for high-quality, collaborative problem-solving, period!'

In other words, the principles which underpin the CSP classroom model are equally applicable at all other levels of educational management – indeed, to management in general – as amply demonstrated in several of the vignettes in Section 3. Bruce highlights three principles in particular:

1. **The need to 'walk the talk'** – by modelling the *review and reflection* process in the *debrief* phase of the CSP cycle (see pages 54–57). As Bruce puts it: 'If we ask others to reflect on their own performance often enough, inevitably we must turn the mirror on ourselves. How well do I listen to the ideas of others? Do I let others know I value their contributions?'

2. **The need to use and/or create a support network ('friends and allies')** – epitomising the *collaborative learning community* component of the CSP cycle (pages 36–43). Here, Bruce introduces the idea of the 'ear' (sometimes known as the 'critical friend'). Such a person can provide invaluable assistance in debriefing sessions, enabling newly trained CSP teachers to 'acknowledge imperfection, reflect on it, and move on to try and do better next time'.

   Of course, as Bruce points out, this process will be much easier to initiate if schools and authorities are able to send groups of colleagues as described, for example, in Rick Lee's vignette (page 105). It will also be much more powerful if these groups contain senior managers who then use the model to create the *collaborative culture* which is so essential for effective support, as described by Anne Callan (page 101).

3. **The need to 'build a constituency'** – through public performances of pupils' work. This relates to the *meaningful context* phase of the CSP cycle (pages 49–51), a powerful way of motivating and engaging pupils by enabling them to see the connection between their school work and the real world outside school. If the opportunity is taken to bring in observers from outside the classroom such as parents, local business people or community leaders, they too can become real 'friends and allies' in taking the programme forward.

In **Article 2: CSP in Your School: Greenhouse or Gobi? Advice for Senior Managers** – under the theme of 'CSP Senior Manager as Master Gardener' Bruce develops a persuasive analogy between school management and gardening. Like 'master gardeners' effective senior managers recognise that they need to apply the following principles if they are to enable their newly trained teachers to develop their CSP skills effectively:

1. **Nurture, don't coerce!** Just as an experienced gardener recognises that no plant can be expected to bear fruit before its time, so effective senior managers recognise that demanding instant results will harm their teachers' chances of success. Even highly motivated and experienced CSP trainees can take three or more years to become fully comfortable with the model.

2. **Work collaboratively with staff**. Senior managers who are prepared to work collaboratively with their staff through the training experience will be in a much better position to help implement the model, for two reasons. First, they will show that they are prepared to share the inevitable risks involved in learning and applying new skills in the classroom. Second, they will demonstrate that they value their staff and their work.

3. **Inspire grassroots interest, not top–down mandate**. To enable CSP to flourish in a school, senior managers need to inspire interest in the training and create a safe environment in which their staff can take risks. Interest is most likely to be generated by seeing competent CSP practitioners in action. And the impact of such an experience back in the school will be all the greater if those who go to observe are themselves experienced teachers, respected by their colleagues. But above all, staff should be allowed to 'own' their decision to train by being given a free choice in the matter.

4. **Select first-round trainees carefully and build in peer support**. The experience of Pete Fox at Gilboa-Conesville (page 66) illustrates the value of having experienced and respected teachers among the first round of training. And just as young plants can benefit from the shelter of other plants, so the collaborative teamwork created among a group of staff who go through training together will be more likely to provide the kind of support needed to develop the newly learned skills effectively (see again Rick Lee's vignette, page 105).

5. **Provide high-quality feedback**. Just like their pupils, newly trained CSP teachers need high-quality feedback on their performance so that they can consolidate their strengths and make corrections where necessary. And as with pupils, high-quality feedback needs to follow two key principles:

   First, it needs to be given in a positive manner and when the recipient is ready, so as to maintain self-esteem and motivation. Second, it needs to be based on clear and agreed criteria. A particular strength of the CSP model is the way in which it clarifies quality criteria into *specific, observable behaviours* (page 39) so that feedback can be highly focused and therefore more valuable.

6. **Share successes and build community**. As Bruce puts it: 'One of the great joys of CSP is the opportunity to watch students produce results that are clear evidence of developing knowledge and skill.' And these opportunities will be all the more productive if they are witnessed by outside observers who can provide authentic 'real world' feedback. By encouraging their teachers to take the risks involved in such activities, and above all by being supportive and emphasising the value that staff are adding to school life through such activities, senior managers will go a long way towards creating the kind of collaborative ethos that is vital to successful implementation of the CSP model.

In **Article 3: Frequently Asked Questions** Bruce provides considered and typically insightful answers to 13 of the commonest questions that he has been asked by some of the hundreds of teachers he has trained over the past 10 years. The questions address three themes: 'grouping students'; 'setting standards'; and 'nurturing a collaborative classroom culture'.

➡ *Theme 1: Grouping students in a CSP classroom* considers the issues of *when* to group; group size; and group composition. Several different ways of organising group membership are described and their relative merits in different situations are discussed.

➡ *Theme 2: Setting standards for students' work* focuses on the key issue of setting and adhering to *quality criteria*. After dealing with the question 'Why set standards for product and process?' Bruce provides detailed advice on setting standards of quality for the *processes* of collaborative work; for the *products* of such work; and for the development of the *Critical Skills* through such work.

➡ *Theme 3: Nurturing a culture of collaboration in the classroom* deals with the following issues: what *is* a 'classroom culture'?; how to build a 'classroom community'; how to make the classroom culture a priority issue for students; the importance of 'walking the talk'; making students more aware of the importance of their individual and collective behaviour; and making sure that desirable behaviours become embedded in the classroom.

Section 5: Lessons for the UK

In this final section of the book, Jo Morrison provides a detailed analysis of four recent and significant Department for Education and Skills documents:

➡ *Delivering Results – A Strategy to 2006*
➡ The Education Bill 2001
➡ *What is the Key Stage 3 National Strategy?*
➡ 14–19 Green Paper: Extending Opportunities, Raising Standards.

Jo demonstrates with great clarity how effectively CSP addresses the key issues identified in all four documents.

For example, the three key objectives identified at the beginning of *A Strategy to 2006* relate to providing children with 'a better foundation for learning'; enabling young people to develop the 'skills, knowledge and personal qualities needed for life and work'; and enabling adults to 'learn, improve their skills and enrich their lives'. As both Jo and John Kerr (Section 2) make clear, CSP provides a uniquely powerful way of meeting these objectives.

Turning to the Education Bill, Jo quotes its mission statement: 'The bill's key theme is innovation... We want to free schools to develop the ideas that will raise standards.' She goes on to point out that 'CSP is replete with "ideas that will raise standards" – perhaps even more than the authors of the Bill had thought possible!'

The Key Stage 3 National Strategy is based on four key principles: *expectations; progression; engagement*; and *transformation*. Clearly, high expectations are an integral feature of the CSP model. As Jo puts it: 'CSP teachers are trained to design challenges which are stretching... They also set and apply rigorous quality criteria...' Equally, through the process of 'reflection and connection' (pages 54–57) CSP provides a powerful way of ensuring that good *progression* in teaching and learning is maintained across Key Stage 3.

The third principle – '*engagement* – promoting approaches to teaching and learning that engage and motivate pupils...' as the Strategy describes it – is also epitomised by CSP challenges. And finally, '*transformation* – strengthening teaching and learning through a programme of professional development and practical support', is an accurate summary of the current CSP training programme, as witnessed to by the several hundred teachers who have undertaken the training over the past three years.

The 14–19 Green Paper opens with the following statement: 'The pace of economic change has not been matched by the pace of change in our education system.' And Jo makes the point that CSP is a conscious – and highly successful – attempt to address this mismatch.

Finally, summarising the relationship between CSP and the DfES's ambitions as portrayed in these four documents, Jo makes the point that: 'CSP practitioners throughout the UK will undoubtedly respond to many of these proposals with delight, and could spearhead the innovation and internalisation that the Government is advocating.'

3. Covering the Route: A Parable for our Times
Bruce Bonney

During the mid-1970s and early 1980s I was a Varsity Boys Basketball coach at our high school. During that period I had many experiences that informed my classroom practice. One incident, however, stands out as a sort of epiphany for me. It involved my players (students) and a school bus driver.

As is the case with many rural communities where every student is transported to school on buses, the drivers and their schedule of routes had enormous influence over many aspects of our school day. So it was that sports coaches in our district were constantly juggling their need for after-school practice time with the desires of the bus drivers to leave the school driveway at precisely 4.50pm. It wasn't unusual to see shower-soaked athletes flying down the hallway, pants,* socks and shoes trailing in the slip-stream, as they rushed to board the bus.

One practice before a particularly important game, my team lingered a bit too long in the gym. Predictably, a mad scramble for the locker room ensued as the kids sprinted to gather their clothes and get to the bus. Meanwhile, I hustled to the driveway to inform the bus driver that my players would be a few seconds late. It must have been 4.49!

As I approached the bus, I could see the driver's hand move for the door handle. No doubt the look on my face was priceless as, with a certain air of detachment, he glanced down at me, turned slowly to face the steering wheel, and, quite deliberately, slammed the door shut.

I was struck dumb! Standing frozen in place, my whistle dangling limp on the lanyard around my neck, I watched as the bus pulled out into the chill December night – empty.

Needless to say, I went ballistic.

The next day I demanded and got a meeting with the principal and the offending driver. I huffed and puffed about meeting the needs of our kids and understanding the role each of us plays in the educational process, and having some flexibility in the system, etc. Through it all the driver calmly picked his nails.

When it came to his turn, the driver looked at us both and laid it on the line.

'Look, fellas,' he said, 'I've been at this job a long time. My job is to cover my route. I get paid to start the bus at 4.50, travel the roads I'm assigned, and get the bus into the garage by 6.15. If the kids or the coaches aren't smart enough or responsible enough to figure out what they have to do to get on the bus, that's their problem. I can't possibly worry about every individual and their difficulties. If they do their job and I do mine, the system will work just fine – they get where they want to go, and I get paid.'

I started to fume – and then it hit me! As I listened to his explanation, I recognized the refrain. It was the bus driver's rationale for covering his syllabus.

For years I had heard the same argument in the staffroom whenever suggestions for reform were offered.

'Look,' they'd say, 'we've been at it for a lot of years. Each of us has a syllabus [route] to cover. We only have so much time to get there. We can't possibly accommodate all the differences in learning styles, family background, intelligences, etc., represented in the kids we serve. We get paid to cover our syllabus [route] and get them ready for the exams in June. Obviously, if the kids don't make it, they must not be capable or responsible enough to get where they need to go. We can't control that.'

So, what do we do?

Early in September we rev up the bus, close the door, and begin covering the route. Oh, we look back occasionally to see how our passengers are doing. Fundamentally, though, we cruise along at our own predetermined pace.

In June, we open the door again, and deliver our passengers to the exams.

If only a few students are to be found in the seats, that's their problem. It's their job to be ready to go along for the ride. Our job is to get those who are capable to the assigned destination on time.

And for those kids who are not ready? Well, like my players that night, they'll just have to find their own way – in the dark.

If this strikes a familiar chord with you, take heart – thanks to Critical Skills, all this can change! Read on…

Section Two: The Critical Skills Programme

John Kerr

The Big Picture

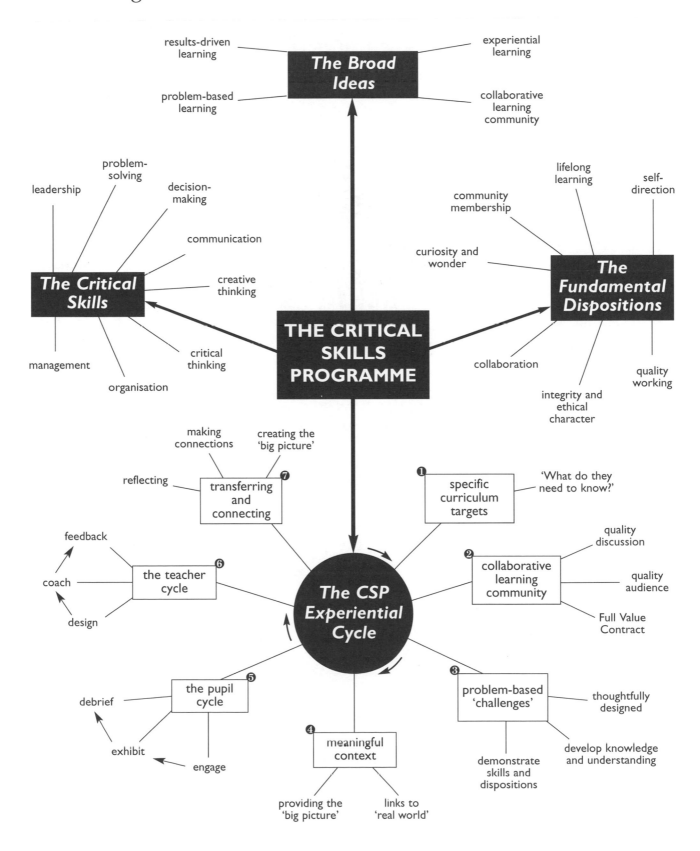

Section Two: The Critical Skills Programme
The Big Picture

Introduction

> 'One of the most pressing issues today is how to foster in pupils a sense of personal investment in their learning.'

Audrey Gibson: 'Re-visioning Revision', page 76

The Critical Skills Programme is practical, effective and realistic, and not only for disaffected pupils, as the comments above might suggest. Nor is it perfect. It depends on the willingness of its practitioners to turn the mirror on themselves and reflect on their own performance by asking the key question: 'Am I doing the best job I can, given the resources?'

This section is based on Chapter 3 of **Leading the Learning School** by Colin Weatherley (Network Educational Press 2000).

> 'Part of the high credibility of our programme is our willingness to acknowledge imperfection, reflect on it, and move on to try and do better next time. Modelling this attitude and pattern of behaviour is central to encouraging it in others.'

Bruce Bonney: 'Staying Alive with CSP', page 123

In the last ten years more has been discovered about how the human brain works than ever before. However, in response to that greater knowledge of, for example, multiple intelligence theory, learning styles and meta-cognition, has our 'delivery' of information changed in schools? CSP does not run counter to the demands of the content-based curriculum. The practitioners and trainers involved in CSP are teachers who still have pupil, parental, education authority and national examination pressures to respond to.

Not only does CSP provide a more effective way of learning within a curriculum and classroom culture still guided by specific targets – whether school, local or national – it also has much to contribute to assessment procedures, discipline and wider life skills. As Brian Speedie comments: 'Critical Skills provided a framework and methodology which was to become of immediate practical use'* (Brian Speedie: 'Using the CSP Model in Curriculum Development', page 97).

* Brian Speedie's article also shows clearly the value of CSP practices in planning and staff development.

Such claims may seem exaggerated, but the purpose of this section is to explain how the Critical Skills Programme provides such a framework, and to describe the impact that it has already had on teachers such as those whose experiences are recounted in Section 3. Several of these experiences will be referred to in this section, to illustrate and illuminate the theoretical model.

How CSP began

In the early 1980s the American education system was widely seen as failing in many ways. Many teachers seemed disillusioned, students disaffected, and the wider community – especially prospective employers – wondered why public money was being spent on public education only to see a product that failed to meet their expectations. In response to these feelings of 'could and should do better', leaders of the education and business communities in New Hampshire met and sought answers to two key questions, the answers to which were to become the bedrock of the CSP model:

* i.e. 'attitudes'.

> **Question 1**
> What skills and dispositions* are vitally important for students to have by the time they leave school in order to be successful in their lives?
>
> **Question 2**
> What skills and dispositions* are currently lacking in the workforce that impede individual and organisational success?

To find answers to these questions the education and business representatives made separate 'wish lists' of what they would like to see happening in their schools. By focusing first on 'skills' surprising agreement was reached between them. The 'skills ... currently lacking in the workforce' were then collated as follows:

Critical skills

- ➡ problem-solving
- ➡ decision-making
- ➡ critical thinking
- ➡ creative thinking
- ➡ communication
- ➡ organisation
- ➡ management
- ➡ leadership.

The group then turned their attention to 'dispositions', and again a surprising degree of consensus was reached:

Fundamental dispositions

- ➡ positive attitude to life-long learning
- ➡ self-direction
- ➡ internal model of quality
- ➡ collaboration
- ➡ integrity and ethical character
- ➡ curiosity and wonder
- ➡ community membership.

It was clear that to achieve these targets, things would have to change to match the needs of a modern, knowledge-based workplace. In our rapidly changing world, school-leavers will be expected to operate flexibly; to develop new skills throughout their working lives; and to operate effectively within collaborative environments. However, despite that reality the education and business communities were conscious of the fact that for the foreseeable future our children will be taught within an education system that remains geared to examination results in both vocational and academic subjects.

As CSP trainers frequently point out: 'If you always do what you've always done, then you'll always get what you've always got'! So, in the attempt to match the demands of the future to the constraints of the present, certain principles concerning the learning process were established. These principles of what education and learning should involve – or *broad ideas* – underpin all CSP thinking. They are:

Broad ideas

➡ experiential learning

➡ a collaborative learning community

➡ results-driven learning

➡ problem-based learning

The experiential cycle

So, having identified the principles behind CSP, how does CSP put these broad ideas into practice?

In essence, the practice of CSP is incorporated into an *experiential learning cycle;* and the diagram below illustrates how the four broad ideas translate into an overall teaching strategy.

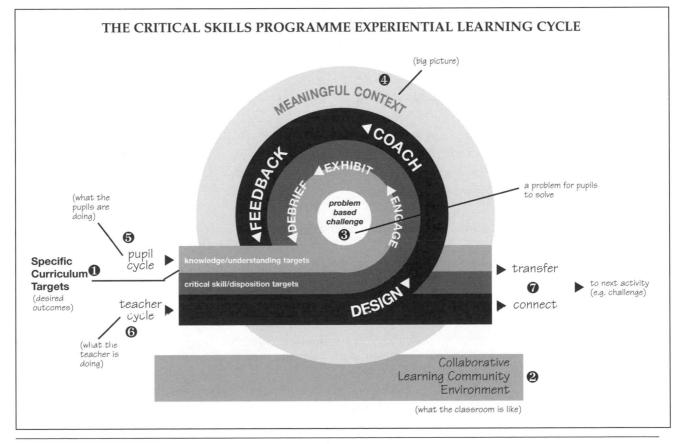

THE CRITICAL SKILLS PROGRAMME EXPERIENTIAL LEARNING CYCLE

Although at first sight the CSP experiential cycle might appear daunting, the rest of this section explains its operation and illustrates this by reference to the experiences of a selection of practitioners, from novices to experts, as described in Section 3.

> 'The Critical Skills Programme was like receiving the 'picture on the lid of a jigsaw' that I have been trying to complete for years. All the theories ... could suddenly be 'fitted' into a structure which made sense.'*

Linda Marshall: 'A Secondary whole-school Perspective' – see page 92

The cycle itself consists of seven parts which link to the four broad ideas, as follows:

1. Specific curriculum targets: What do the pupils have to know?

Specific curriculum targets – or desired outcomes – are at the core of the *challenge* (see No. 3) and link strongly to the broad idea of *results-driven learning*.

2. The collaborative learning community environment: What is a CSP classroom like?

The collaborative learning community environment provides a definition of how the CSP classroom helps to achieve the learning and teaching goals within the cycle.*

3. Problem-based 'challenges': Complex, open-ended problems for pupils to solve

The concept of challenges links clearly to the broad idea of problem-based learning. Challenges require pupils to *engage* in the process, *exhibit* their work and experience *debriefing* (that is, review, reflection and feedback) as a key part of the process.

4. Meaningful context: Why are we doing this?

The meaningful context is a crucial part of the CSP philosophy. Without the awareness of the 'big picture', how can pupils see where their contribution fits in? Without the big picture, what is the purpose of what they do?*

5. The pupil cycle: What the pupils are doing

The experiential cycle shows how work done or situations experienced lead to the acquisition and application of new knowledge, skills and attitudes. Pupils must demonstrate visible learning in operation, be that knowledge and understanding, *critical skills* or *fundamental dispositions*.

6. The teacher cycle: What the teacher does

In the CSP experiential cycle the teacher is designer, coach and adviser, providing feedback to help pupils' learning. New roles such as these demand new skills and the refining of old ones. To paraphrase Pete Fox (page 69), CSP requires 'old dogs to learn new tricks but also reminds us that old tricks can still work for young dogs.'*

7. Transferring and Connecting: Making sense of it all.

Having completed a challenge, it is essential to give pupils time to reflect on what they have learnt and see how it connects to their general learning progress, both as

---

* Many others have made similar comments; e.g. Liz Grierson, a primary school deputy head, said: ' "Critical Skills" is what we've been searching for for years – a very practical and structured way of bringing all the brain-based learning ideas together.'

* Linda Marshall's vignette (page 92) serves as encouragement to anyone launching CSP in their school and makes the point that 'it is much easier to set up a collaborative community if you work in one'.

* 'The purposes of activities are shared with pupils and care is taken to explain work to them within the context of what they already know and can do.' (**How Good is Our School? Self-evaluation using Performance Indicators**, HMSO 1996, P.I. 3.1: 'Quality of the teaching process')

* See Forrest Howie's comments that 'CSP is a development and not a revolution' (page 73). And in 'Critical Signs and Clear Portents' (page 105) Rick Lee reinforces the point that in many ways CSP synthesises existing good practice into a holistic approach.

Transforming Teaching & Learning

individuals and as a community of learners. Do certain skills need further attention? Is their learning community functioning as well as it should?

1. Specific curriculum targets

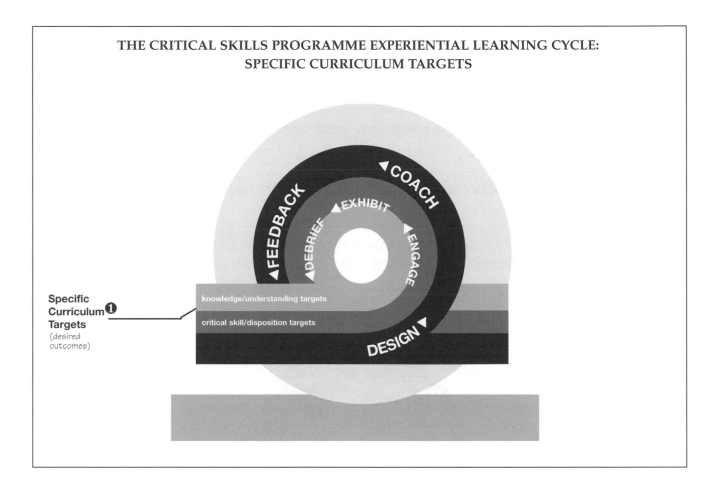

THE CRITICAL SKILLS PROGRAMME EXPERIENTIAL LEARNING CYCLE:
SPECIFIC CURRICULUM TARGETS

Specific Curriculum ❶ Targets (desired outcomes)

knowledge/understanding targets

critical skill/disposition targets

FEEDBACK DEBRIEF EXHIBIT COACH ENGAGE DESIGN

All too often CSP practitioners have faced comments such as: 'Yes, it's a good idea but we have syllabuses to get through and exams to present for.' So do we all! None of us would be involved with CSP if it meant disadvantaging our pupils by turning them into 'guinea pigs'.

CSP challenges are very much content driven. But riding on the 'locomotive' of content come all the extra skills/dispositional material – and the opportunity to process learned information in a way which leads to real learning gains, as opposed to the mere presentation of information to pupils on the assumption that in so doing, course content has been covered. How much 'conventional' teaching time is spent re-teaching because pupils have not really learned the material first time around?

Although pupils cover a lot of content in school, how long do they spend processing this information – allowing their brains, their conscious and subconscious minds, to link new learning to old, to see how the small lesson links to the bigger picture of a whole syllabus, how it relates to their lives and ambitions?

When given a task requiring performance – that is a *challenge* – pupils are required to put their knowledge to work. Obviously the acquisition and processing of the knowledge is a vital ingredient and any presentation by pupils could not happen

* See, for example, the passage on 'thinking and learning' in **Leading the Learning School** (pages 23–27).

without it. An added advantage is that by *using* the information, not just *acquiring* it, the depth of understanding is enhanced.*

But CSP curriculum targets are much more than a collection of desirable learning outcomes. The *CSP Level 1 Training Manual* (1998) puts it succinctly when it states:

> 'Learning standards (i.e. curriculum targets) are the outcomes, frameworks, or desired results – set at the classroom, school, or national level – that define what we want our students to know, understand, do, and be like while they are in school, and when they have completed their schooling.'

2. Creating a collaborative classroom learning community

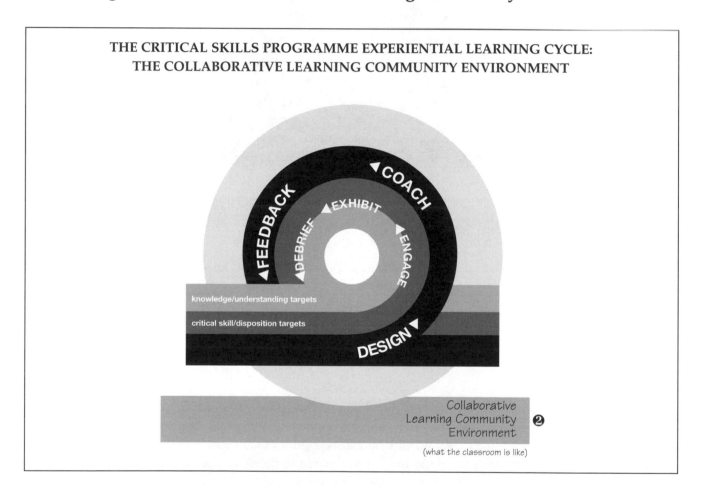

THE CRITICAL SKILLS PROGRAMME EXPERIENTIAL LEARNING CYCLE: THE COLLABORATIVE LEARNING COMMUNITY ENVIRONMENT

FEEDBACK • DEBRIEF • EXHIBIT • COACH • ENGAGE • DESIGN

knowledge/understanding targets

critical skill/disposition targets

Collaborative Learning Community Environment ❷

(what the classroom is like)

* Rick Lee (page 105) describes the benefits that a Full Value Contract had on 'the quality of our conversation and the respect we gave each other in debate and towards our presentations.'

Creating teams or communities based on differences between individuals will inevitably lead to some tensions, and eventually basic operational rules will be needed. However, CSP practice tends to delay the emergence or creation of 'community rules' until pupils have appreciated the need for them – and that usually happens only after the setting of a challenge which requires collaboration for success. Pupils need to see why they should collaborate. Once that realisation has emerged, progress can be made towards the ground rules, known in CSP as *The Full Value Contract*.*

Towards a Full Value Contract

The Full Value Contract (FVC) is a phrase, tool and a philosophy which permeates CSP. Without it, little of value would be achieved. It is a set of basic rules that everyone in the class, including the teacher, agrees to follow. Once established, it soon becomes a very effective way of promoting appropriate behaviour and effective learning in the classroom. However, the FVC is much more than procedural do's and don'ts.

A useful definition of the FVC from the *CSP Level 1 Training Manual* is:

'... a social contract that helps to create a safe place to be for each individual, while the notion of 'full value' refers to assigning full value to others rather than discounting them.'

Only when pupils have had sufficient experience of challenges and the difficulties and frustrations that come from inefficient organisation, will they see the usefulness of the FVC as, to use more conventional terminology, the importance of 'basic ground rules' emerges.

Agreement within the group is essential to the FVC, but so is the need for it to be seen as useful and relevant; hence the need for it to emerge from some initial group experiences. For a teacher to 'announce' it is clearly unproductive and in practice the FVC should emerge as a result of working through one or more challenges, rather than preceding them, so that the need for such a contract is appreciated by all.

At the core of the FVC, then, is recognition of the need to work together, to stick to certain safety and behavioural guidelines, to give and take feedback, and to change styles of behaviour when appropriate. In essence the contract is summarised in the *CSP Level 1 Manual* thus:

'All members of the group agree to:
- play and work hard
- play and work safely*
- play and work fairly.'

* Note that 'safely' covers emotional as well as physical safety.

Within CSP certain *tools* are used to assist the emergence of the FVC. These tools are always introduced within a practical context – often a *challenge** – so that pupils, and teachers, see their relevance.

* See page 44.

The word 'tool' is used to describe a process which facilitates the creation and operation of a collaborative learning community. The names of these tools may sound too 'American' for easy importation to UK classrooms. Time will no doubt tell! But names can be changed – it is the processes involved that are essential to the building of the community.

The first tools* to be described are:
- quality discussion standards
- the sweep
- the thumb tool
- quality audience standards.

* Rick Lee (page 105) provides a vivid description of the use of many of these tools in the training programme.

Others will follow, namely:

→ the carousel brainstorm

→ the IP3 tool

→ chunking the challenge.

Quality discussion standards

Under pressure of time and the realisation of the expectations put upon them, pupils begin to realise that tasks must be allocated and performed efficiently. Collaboration is vital and therefore so is *quality discussion* of these tasks.

Pupils soon realise that time-wasting is not a good idea; nor is duplication of effort. They therefore need to communicate effectively with each other in order to work effectively. In fact, the importance of efficient and effective communication within a group can be embedded within a challenge:

'I then gave them the following *challenge* which required them to work in groups to create a poster, a statement and a new set of rules which would be useful to a new member of their team. They had to explain what their values were, and what would be expected of a new team member'* (Anne Callan: 'Using CSP with Teachers', page 102).

* Anne Callan not only describes how challenges and tools are applicable to pupils' learning but also how these techniques facilitate staff working together on whole-school issues.

Having established the need for quality discussion, pupils can be asked the key question:

'What will a quality discussion look like and sound like?'

Pupils are given a very short time to decide their answers. The class teacher has a decision to make at this point and the answer will largely depend on the aptitude, age and attitude of the pupils: should the roles within the group be allocated by the teacher or should s/he leave it to the pupils themselves to realise the need for recorders, facilitators, reporters, etc. and then allocate these tasks among and so on themselves?

The sweep

Within the group, and the class as a whole, the *sweep tool* can be used to ensure that everyone has an input to the task.

When the time allocated for the task is complete a further short period should be given for the groups to prioritise their answers. The sweep tool requires each group reporter to give *one* only of their group's suggested *quality discussion standards* (criteria). With each member of each group contributing to the decisions in the final list of standards, the sweep is a device which ensures inclusion and a sense of ownership within the whole class.

Of course, teachers should remember that they too are part of the classroom community and so are as entitled as the pupils to make contributions to the development of the community's ground rules.

It may be thought that all this sounds idealistically impractical and that some pupils will actively oppose the process; but what is the alternative? Will these same pupils be more or less willing to accept rules imposed by the teacher? Do they have ownership of those rules? Is resistance to imposed authority more or less likely than to agreed rules mutually arrived at?

> 'For some pupils, defying me was a way of asserting themselves. Thus, there were at least as many reasons not to follow instructions and do badly as there were to do their best.'
>
> Audrey Gibson, page 77

However, opposition and disagreement are part of any community and in CSP they can be turned to the advantage of the group by using ...

The thumb tool

Once the suggestions from each group have been listed, it's time to ask a question:

➡ 'Does everyone understand what each suggestion means?'

Vague terms such as 'co-operate'; 'showing respect for others'; or 'listening carefully' must be clarified. One of the core features of CSP is the 'looks like, sounds like' maxim, this is:

➡ 'What does respect and co-operation look like and sound like? What will you see and hear if people are showing respect and/or co-operating?'

In CSP such *specific observable behaviours* are vital.

Having clarified the suggestions from the groups, another question can be asked:

➡ 'Can everyone in the group operate within these rules?'

The thumb tool now comes into operation. For each of the suggested rules the pupils are asked to give one of three different thumb positions.

✓ a thumbs-up means 'Yes, I'm happy with this rule.'
✓ a horizontal thumb means 'I'm not all that happy but I'll agree to go along with it.'
✓ a thumbs-down means 'I can't agree to this rule.'

Anyone with a thumb down must give a reason for their objection, and a real discussion can then take place with the pupil(s) as to why they find the rule difficult. This discussion can be calm and constructive, since the rule itself has not been broken. Pupils do not feel defensive, because they are being asked for their opinion about how they should behave – and why – maybe for the first time ever in a classroom! Pupils can then be asked for alternative suggestions.

After the discussion has finished, a final version of the quality discussion standards can be made. By using the sweep and the thumb tool the opinions and attitudes of the class as a whole are quickly established. The agreed list of requirements can then be publicly displayed and used as an easy reminder of appropriate behaviour.

It may seem that this will take too much additional time, but how much time is wasted in enforcing 'school rules' on reluctant pupils? With a set of genuinely agreed standards of behaviour it's easy to remind pupils that they have departed from their agreement. A reasonable discussion start is to ask why they have broken their agreement – a much more personal and reflective question than a threatening accusation which often leads to an impasse or reluctant conformity.

The quality audience

Since the completion of a challenge is normally marked by a public demonstration of achievement – often a performance by groups in front of their peers – another important tool for effective collaborative work is the means by which the standards for a *quality audience* are set. Given that all members of the learning community will be performers *and* members of the audience, the whole class is asked the key question:

➡ 'What will a quality audience look like and sound like?'

The outcome of such a quality discussion might include:

Transforming Teaching & Learning

Putting the Full Value Contract into action

Some typical comments from pupils once they have applied the Full Value Contract demonstrate its effectiveness:

As in life, pupils need to learn how to operate effectively and productively when out of 'friendly waters'. Once again, teachers can highlight just how practically useful the CSP tools of quality discussion and quality audience can be.* By agreeing to play safely – which also implies *emotional safety* – pupils can see that while they are constrained to show respect for others, the bonus is that they themselves are equally valued.

Having established the general outline of the FVC, pupils and teachers should now move towards a more precise, clearer definition of what 'Full Value' means to them in terms of specific, observable behaviours. And once again CSP provides a useful 'tool' to facilitate this process – specifically:

* Several headteachers have reported that 'Can I have a quality audience please?' has proved an extremely effective way of gaining pupils' attention at assemblies.

*The carousel brainstorm and distillation tool**

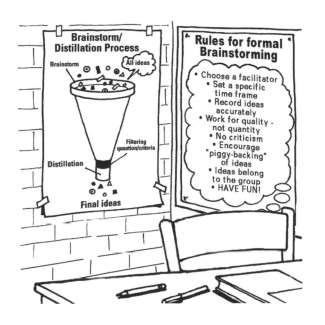

To participate in a carousel effectively, pupils must have explicit instructions. Even if they have brainstormed before, it is always useful to remind them of the basic rules, which should also be on display in the classroom.

Pupils are then presented with a series of questions which direct them towards thinking about what their learning environment should be like:

➡ What will our classroom look like and sound like if we all play **fair**?

* The use of this tool is described in several of the Section 3 vignettes, e.g. Audrey Gibson's (see page 79); Heather Swinson's (page 84); Anne Callan's (page 101).

➡ What will our classroom look like and sound like if we all play **hard**?

➡ What will our classroom look like and sound like if we all play **safe, physically**?

➡ What will our classroom look like and sound like if we all play **safe, emotionally**?

Each group is issued with a different coloured marker pen and given limited time to brainstorm responses to one of the above questions on a flipchart sheet. Then they 'carousel' to the next flipchart sheet, still with their identifying colour marker. The group recorders can then either add to (but not alter) previous groups' responses, or tick existing ones that they agree with. Once the groups have had a chance to respond to all four of the above questions they return to their original stations and go through the *distillation* process by asking two questions:

1. Is the description listed on the chart *relevant and significant* in terms of the original question?

2. Is the description *specific and observable?*

By using a sweep again, the distilled ideas of each group can be collected.

Transforming Teaching & Learning

A short period of discussion within the groups follows about the distillation responses listed on the sweep chart and then the thumb tool is used to search for the areas of agreement or disagreement. Finally, an agreed list of behaviours, unique to that class, is written up neatly and subsequently displayed on the wall whenever that class is in the room.

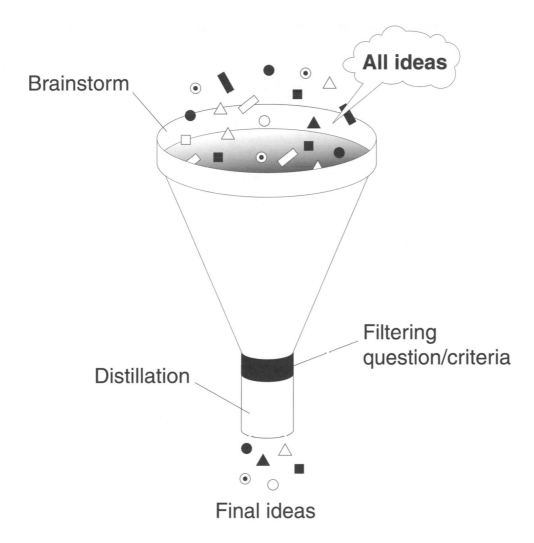

Brainstorm

All ideas

Filtering question/criteria

Distillation

Final ideas

(NB: The filter funnel diagram can also be used to illustrate the principle behind brainstorming, which is to take account of different learning styles and allow pupils to hear, read and visualise instructions according to their learning preferences.)

The effective development of a Full Value Contract certainly requires teaching skills of a high order but its existence means that the teacher has a very powerful tool for classroom management, discipline and assessment, since all activities are agreed, not imposed, and can be seen and heard in operation.

From time to time the FVC might need reviewing and altering – for example at the beginning of a new term; if new pupils join the class; or if it is clear that agreement is not unanimous, that is the community is not united.

3. The challenge – a problem for pupils to solve

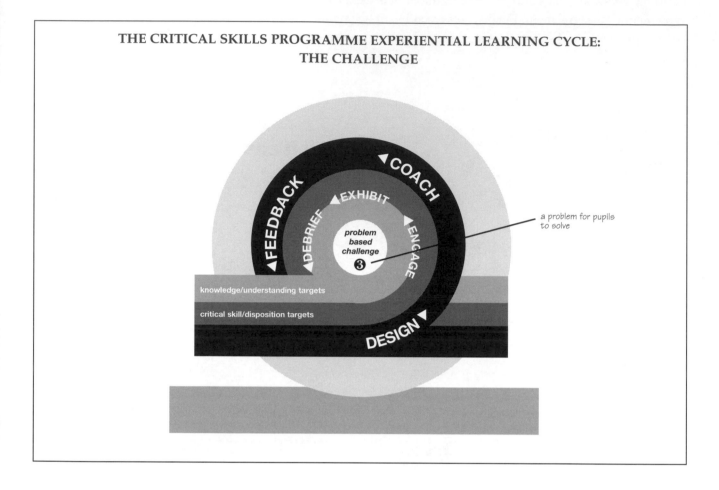

THE CRITICAL SKILLS PROGRAMME EXPERIENTIAL LEARNING CYCLE:
THE CHALLENGE

a problem for pupils
to solve

* Subsection 4, 'The
Meaningful Context'
(page 49) provides
further information
about challenges and,
in particular, how they
fit into the experiential
learning cycle.

At the heart of the experiential learning cycle lies the *challenge*,* which can vary enormously in complexity and content. Challenges essentially represent *problem-based learning* and are designed to pose a problem for pupils – or staff – to solve as individuals, in small groups, or as a full learning community – even sometimes as a whole-school!

A classroom challenge should be designed to:

➡ enable pupils to achieve *specific curriculum targets*

➡ provide *clarity and confidence* about the learning task

➡ promote *understanding through performance*

➡ cater for different *styles of decision-making*

➡ cater for different *styles of thinking and learning*

➡ provide regular opportunities to use and develop *multiple intelligences*.

These features are identified in the following annotated extracts from a lower secondary science challenge.

Transforming Teaching & Learning

ACADEMIC CHALLENGE (PUPIL VERSION)
Lower Secondary: Science

(ii) provides clarity about the learning task

(iii) i.e. different styles of thinking and decision-making

(viii) promoting collaborative learning

Question/Issue: How are whales adapted to their environment?

Challenge Description: With the help of your teacher, arrange yourselves into well balanced teams of three. Plan and create a colourful, informative, easy-to-understand bulletin board display of your own unique design about a particular whale species that interests you. Your display should reveal accurate information in response to each of the following focus questions:

1. What is your whale species 'like' (its unique physiology)?

2. What does your whale species 'do' (its different behaviours)?

3. Where in the ocean does your whale live; what environmental conditions exist there?

4. How do you think the three questions above might be related?

To assist in your planning of this project, please turn in a project planning sheet at the end of today showing the work schedule for each member of the team for the remainder of the week. You are expected to implement this plan.

Your team will have three class periods to prepare your bulletin board. Be prepared to present your final product on Friday at 2.00pm. All members of the team will be expected to be able to answer questions about your bulletin board and whale species.

Product Criteria: (Bulletin Board)

(iv) promoting understanding through performance

(v) catering for different styles of thinking and learning

(vi) using multiple intelligences

(viii) developing collaborative work skills

(vii) generating high expectations

(ix) the focus of regular, formative assessment

Process Criteria: (Targeted Indicators)
Knowledge/Understanding - understands and applies scientific concepts

Skill/Disposition: Organization - rations resources (time, people and materials) effectively

---

ACADEMIC CHALLENGE (TEACHER VERSION)
Lower Secondary: Science

Question/Issue: } as per pupil
Challenge Description: } version

(iia) generated in the process of 'chunking the challenge' (page 53); give clarity and confidence

Product Criteria: (Bulletin Board)
Form Criteria
● Colourful - 3–5 different colours are used effectively
● Informative - gives viewer important information about the subject
● Easy to understand - audience can accurately interpret information
● Design of the board is unique - does not look exactly like that of any other team

Content Criteria
● Each focus question is addressed directly
● All information about the whale species is accurate
● Focus concepts (behaviour, physiology, environment etc.) used appropriately
● Reveals connections between physiology, behaviour and environment

Process Criteria: (Targeted Key Indicators)
Knowledge/Understanding Target: 'Show secure knowledge and understanding of the ways in which living things interact with their environment.'
Specific observable behaviour - appropriate use of the focus concepts in response to questions

Skill/Disposition Target: Organization
- **optimizing time and resources**
- **employing organizational tools, reviewing and revising plans**
Specific observable behaviour - each team will submit and implement a project planning sheet detailing the work schedule for each member during the week

(i) the desired learning outcomes to achieve specific curriculum targets

(ix) used in 'debriefing' (page 54) as the focus of regular formative assessment

---

Challenges fall into three main types:

* A sample scenario challenge is shown on page 50.

➡ *Academic challenges* are most readily found in classrooms where pupils work within a team to achieve and demonstrate specifically targeted skills and attitudes. The challenge always contains clear criteria for success in terms of form and content, the latter arising directly from the area of study being followed by the pupils.

➡ *Scenario challenges** also require pupils to work within teams, but are more focused on a 'problem to solve'. Often involving some role-play and imagination, pupils operate within 'real life' scenarios and constraints such as financial, time or target deadlines. The final product of this sort of challenge may only be the group's proposal involving planning, explanation and role-play, but nevertheless, the constraints they have worked within were real.

➡ *Real life challenges.* A sample real life challenge is shown below.

REAL LIFE PROBLEM
(read to students)

Primary (K-2) 5–7 years old

Dear Students

I am Miss Dottie from the Cackling Hen Nursery School. I care for small children who could really use the help of some bigger kids like you. I was speaking to your teacher, Ms Penney, and she tells me that you are a very caring class with many good ideas. I sure hope so because I have a problem that I would like you to help me solve.

In my nursery school I have 15 children who are only 3 or 4 years old. They need help in learning about our community. I want my students to learn something about the people in our community who have important jobs. We need to learn how these people help us to have better lives.

I know that I cannot take my children to see all those people in our community who have important jobs, and I can't think of any way to have all those people come to one place to meet my children.

I do have one idea that might work. That is why I need your help. I would like to bring my children to your classroom for a visit. I would like each of you to find out about a person in our community who has an important job which makes our lives better. When my class and I come for our visit, I would like you to teach my children about the people and the jobs you have learned about.

Please remember that the children in my care are very young. They learn best when they can see, touch, smell, or taste things. If you could find a way to let them play with something that will teach them about the person and the job that you select, I am sure my kids will really enjoy themselves.

Will your class help me out?

Sincerely,

Ms. Dottie
Teacher, Cackling Hen Nursery School

A *real life challenge* is defined as 'Work which is necessitated by a real problem in need of a real solution that has the potential for actual implementation at the class, school, community, regional, national or global level' (*A Sampler of Critical Skills Challenges*, Leading EDGE LLC 2000).

That may sound overly ambitious, but such challenges are well within the scope of many places of learning once CSP practices and philosophy become established.* As Heather Swinson states:

* Both Brian Speedie (page 98) and Anne Callan (page 102) also illustrate how challenges can have very direct application to the here and now.

> 'I wanted to involve the boys in 'experiential learning' by designing a real life challenge which would hook them and sustain their interest over a period of time.'

Heather Swinson: 'A Special Needs Teacher's Experience', page 84

Pupils must meet criteria acceptable to real people in the real world. For example, a whole year group could collaborate on arranging a Parents Open Evening, with tasks ranging from catering, planning, entertaining, designing, communicating, ... the list of collaborative activities is almost endless, the risk of failure is real, and so the buzz of successful achievement is high!*

*See, for example, Rick Lee's vivid description of the scenario challenge he and his colleagues encountered in their Level 1 training (page 107)!

Challenges require careful and thoughtful design, based around the key question: 'What are the desired results of the activity?'

Such a clear understanding of intended outcomes greatly benefits the structure of the challenge and its assessment, as will be seen later.

Depending on the desired learning outcomes, pupils will be focused on a specific area of knowledge and understanding and a specific skill or attitude, but they will also be reinforcing their collaborative learning community. But what dynamics make up these communitites?

Within every group differing styles and preferences regarding learning, working, organising and the importance placed on interpersonal skills will be encountered. Members of the group will have different behavioural needs, differing levels of self-esteem and differing learning styles. How, then, can a collaborative community be created? How can a balanced team be created?

At first 'ice-breaking' games can be used to break down some barriers; and by asking pupils if they prefer to work with text or diagrams, and how important new ideas are to them, some preliminary sorting into groups can be achieved.* However, CSP provides a more accurate 'tool' for recognising these differences in learning styles and, more importantly, turning them to advantage. It is called the IP3 tool.

* For a fuller description of this procedure see **Leading the Learning School**, pages 77–78.

Using the IP3 tool

IP3 stands for the initials 'I – P– P– I'. These letters represent four basic styles of thinking and decision-making. The tool can be used to assist the creation of learning communities but it also helps teachers and organisers to gain an understanding of how any group works. It helps to identify different styles of thinking and decision-making, and leads all of us to consider the effects that these differences have on the ways people work together.

The 'I' in IP3 stands for **'ideas' people who**	➡ are *creative* ➡ look for *choice and options* ➡ dislike *rigid rules* ➡ prefer activities like *brainstorming* and *debriefing*
The first 'P' in IP3 stands for **'people' people who**	➡ are concerned with *group dynamics* and *relationships* ➡ are motivated to find common elements of *co-operation* and *understanding* ➡ enjoy *small group discussions* and *positive debriefing*
The second 'P' in IP3 stands for **'product' people who**	➡ like *clear targets* ➡ need to achieve *high-quality results* ➡ often fail to consider fully the interpersonal consequences of their *'drive'* ➡ like setting *success criteria* and *debriefing*
The third 'P' in IP3 stands for **'process' people who**	➡ aim to bring *order and discipline* to the group ➡ like to establish *logical and effective procedures* ➡ like *rituals* and *debriefing*

CSP, IP3 and different styles of thinking and learning

Much has been heard over recent years about differentiation, and a common strategy in this regard is to differentiate between faster and slower learners. But is not an important factor in learning also the preferred learning styles? IP3 demonstrates that we all respond in differing ways to different learning tasks and environments.

By asking *'What have we got to do?'* pupils who respond more readily to 'ideas' and 'product' become involved as ideas of possible forms and thoughts of a product are ignited.

When considering *'How are we going to do it?'* pupils who think more in terms of 'process' come into their own. And to achieve collaboration, 'people' people will gravitate towards ensuring a working relationship among all members so that the goal can be reached.

* See the annotated Academic Challenge on page 45.

But remember – each team or group should be a composite of differing styles. It may be that none of these operations is stated explicitly, or even realised, but within the group these disparate elements complement each other unconsciously.

* Bruce Bonney's company, Leading EDGE LLC, has produced pro-forma sheets based on the IP3 model which enable teachers to design and debrief challenges in a way which caters for and encourages all four of these style preferences – see, for example, **Leading the Learning School**, page 166.

Well constructed challenges* allow for such differentiation, and experienced challenge designers will deliberately target different learning styles within the overall challenge so as to 'include' all styles, thereby assisting not only collaboration but also the raising of self-esteem – a crucial element in ensuring that pupils are willing to engage in the learning process.*

At first teachers may use 'impressionistic' means of establishing group mix based on IP3 principles, but more accurate definitions are often achieved by using the 'Decision-Making Styles' questionnaire which is provided in Level 1 CSP training. It is important to stress that we all have elements of all of IP3 within us – but it is our 'bottom line', that is our favoured style, that we tend to fall back on in moments of stress.

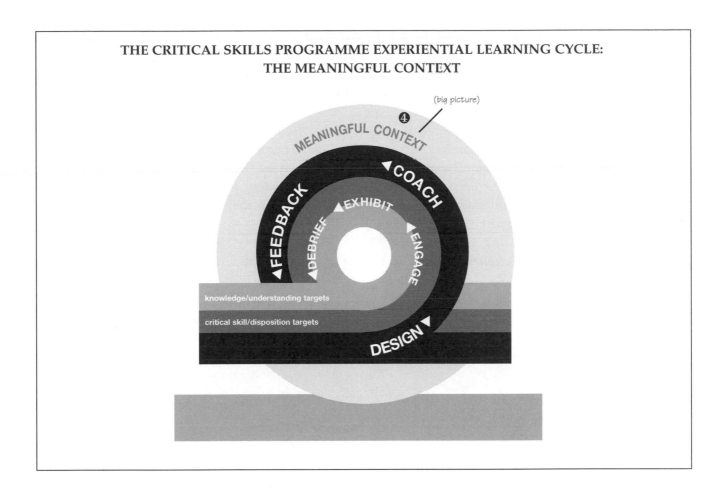

**THE CRITICAL SKILLS PROGRAMME EXPERIENTIAL LEARNING CYCLE:
THE MEANINGFUL CONTEXT**

4. The meaningful context

How often do pupils engage in work only because they have been told to? How often are teachers prepared to meet the challenge from troublesome pupils who say they don't see why they should engage in a task – usually phrased as 'What's the point of this?' *

* Audrey Gibson's pupils clearly started with this attitude! (See page 77.)

An essential element in the CSP model is the 'big picture'. Pupils must see the relevance of the challenge – how it relates to the world they live in; how it fits into a course being followed; how it links to work done; and how it leads on to further development.

Such a focus also has implications for teaching and challenge design. Designers must think about the development of their pupils, the direction in which their teaching is going, and make explicit in any work where in the map of progression the tasks asked of the pupil fit in. That is the *meaningful context*.

Each type of challenge – *academic*, *scenario* and *real life* – has its meaningful context or 'big picture' location.

Academic challenges are designed to integrate with work being done by pupils to meet the demands of school, regional or national syllabuses. However, rather than pupils experiencing subjects as though they were rabbits pulled from a magician's hat – or as travellers entering a dark tunnel with no vision of context apart from areas of illumination lit by the teacher's torch – pupils are made aware of how each challenge integrates with the big picture. For many, this just becomes part of normal school work but at that level the work is nevertheless meaningful.

Within these activities there is another level of 'meaningful' which may not become obvious to many pupils until later. For they are asked to work within 'real life' constraints, such as time limitations, and they need to learn to organise themselves as the teacher withdraws from the traditional 'leader' model.

To develop this meaningful context further the pupils must at least learn to co-operate – and hopefully collaborate – with others in their group who may differ markedly in their own preferred learning and decision-making styles. Ultimately their own 'cool' is on the line when the time of presentation and debrief arrives, if they present work which they perceive as failing the group, the class or the criteria they accepted when the challenge was 'chunked'.*

* See 'Chunking the challenge' on page 53.

Scenario challenges move the idea of meaningful context into a more realistic setting. Challenges are designed around problems to solve which try to increase the 'real feel' of an area of study by putting pupils in real life or fictional roles. Such challenges often require pupils to exercise imagination and creativity in simulating the conditions of the role or 'scenario', as shown in the following example from a history course for 11-year-old pupils in New York State.

| Knowledge 'Standard' – speak and write to transmit information. World History – use a variety of intellectual skills to demonstrate an understanding of major ideas, eras and themes. | **Scenario Challenge**
A Roman Dig | Skill/Disposition 'Standard' – Problem solving – constructing and employing problem solving strategies |

Middle School
ELA/Soc. Studies

The Setting

You are a team of highly trained archaeologists. You've recently made an amazing discovery and have 'uncovered' an ancient Roman town close to the city of Rome itself. Immediately upon discovering the site, you contacted your employer, the curators at the famous Delaware County museum located in Delhi, NY, and told them the good news via a satellite link.

Since your employers had been looking to expand their museum in order to promote more tourism in Delhi, they were very excited about your find.

Your sponsors requested that you make an excavation of the site and return home with artefacts and other knowledge about life in ancient Rome.

The Challenge

Your challenge is to present your findings to a panel from the museum. Your job is to clearly describe the culture of the time period you have excavated. Your sponsors want to know how people of this time period lived, and how their lives were similar or different from ours. Your sponsors know that visitors to museums are most interested in the topics listed below. If your sponsors are going to be at all interested in what you have, you should address all of these topics in your presentation.

- **home life**: roles of family members, what homes looked like, contents of a home, marriage customs, religious beliefs;
- **the military**: how it was run, weapons used, who conquered whom;
- **technology**: what inventions of the time helped make life easier or more comfortable for the people;
- **the land itself**: what land forms affected them (helped them or hurt them);
- **rulers or government**: how the people interacted with the rulers or government, how much did it affect the people's every day lives;
- **entertainment**: what did these people do for enjoyment.

As part of your presentation, please be sure to include:

- a 'blueprint' drawing of the town you've uncovered;
- at least two artefacts from each area of discovery;
- a 3–5 minute explanation of the findings from each of the areas. Please indicate what the artefacts are, what they were used for, and how people of today might see a connection to their own lives;
- a projection of funds needed to continue research for next year.

This presentation will determine whether grant money of $1,000,000 will be given to you. This money will be used not only to continue your research in Italy, but to oversee the building of a new wing at the museum where your artefacts will be displayed.

A similar challenge will be familiar to those teachers who have experienced the second phase of Level 1 CSP training. The challenge is also about a 'dig' and although it is a fictional scenario, the pressures, stresses and ultimately the feelings of relief and triumph are all very real!*

* See Rick Lee's description of this challenge (page 107).

The third level of challenge – the *real life challenge* – has at its core a very meaningful context. By presenting real challenges to be met, overcome and presented to real people, with real expectations and with real possibilities of failure, this context is very meaningful indeed!* Again, the underlying skills and dispositions which are part of the process may not be obvious at all times to all pupils but they are part of real life co-operation and collaboration, just as they were with the first challenge they encountered.

* See vignettes 3, 4, 8 and 10.

5. The Pupil Cycle: What do pupils have to do?

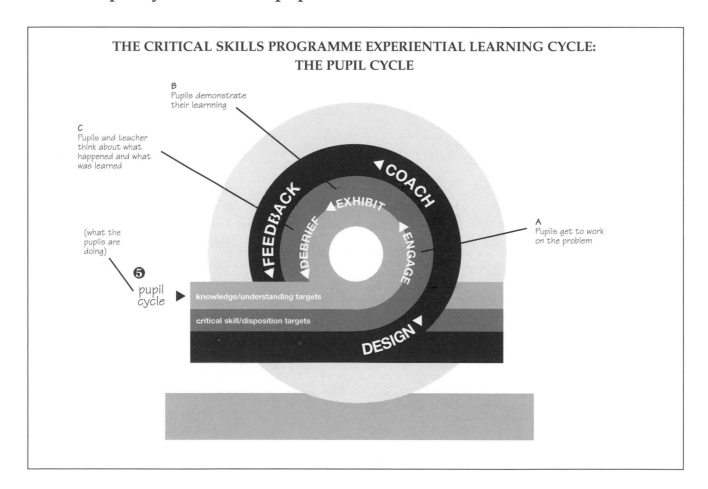

THE CRITICAL SKILLS PROGRAMME EXPERIENTIAL LEARNING CYCLE:
THE PUPIL CYCLE

B
Pupils demonstrate their learnning

C
Pupils and teacher think about what happened and what was learned

(what the pupils are doing)

⑤ pupil cycle ▶

FEEDBACK ◀ ◀DEBRIEF ◀EXHIBIT ◀COACH ◀ENGAGE DESIGN▼

A
Pupils get to work on the problem

knowledge/understanding targets

critical skill/disposition targets

What the pupils do: A – 'Engage'

Using the first challenge

The first challenge presented is often a team challenge which requires each team to create a group identity and present it as a graphic and logo; to introduce the personalities within each group; and also proclaim their new group identity to the rest of the class. In so doing two 'first principles' are established.

First of all the idea of a structured challenge has been presented. Secondly, the foundations of a collaborative learning community have been laid. But how exactly is the challenge used to produce the desired outcomes, which in this case are familiarisation with some important CSP tools and the emergence of a class Full Value Contract? To do this, two more important CSP tools are used, namely:

➡ the check-in

➡ 'chunking the challenge'

The check-in

The *check-in* is a tool most commonly used at the beginning of a day or lesson. Seated in a circle so that each can see and be seen by the others, each member of the class – including the teacher/'coach' – can reflect and comment on whatever they feel is relevant to them or the class since they last met. It can be entirely open or it can be more structured, with comments and/or questions directed at previous learning so as to establish good understanding of previous work before new learning activities are introduced.

Participants also have the opportunity to 'pass' but, if regularly repeated, that also provides feedback to the teacher/coach who might decide it is appropriate to investigate if the passer feels distanced from the group. For some 'product' people* this is one of the hardest tasks to perform, but it also constitutes a reminder that learning to accommodate others is essential in any community.

> **TEAM CHALLENGE (EXTRACT)**
>
> **Question/Issue:** Who are we? What are our strengths as individuals and as a group? How can we organize ourselves to work together productively?
>
> **Challenge Description:** With the help of your teacher, create balanced teams of four.* These teams will work together to solve Challenges for some time, so try to ensure that you have a good mix of thinking styles in your team.
>
> You will have one hour to prepare a presentation of no more than 5 minutes in which you introduce the members of your team to the rest of the class. Your presentation should include:
> - your names
> - some information about each of you (eg family, interests, things you have done, things you would like to do)
> - one or two behaviours that your team thinks will be most important for you all to show if you are to meet the Challenges you will be presented with over the next few weeks.
> - what strengths you have as individuals and as a team that will help you in your work
>
> You should also produce a logo that includes the information in your presentation, and a name that you feel sums up who you are and what you intend to do.
>
> As you organize your team, please be careful to stay within the comfort level of all team members.

* See 'Using the IP3 tool' on pages 47–48.

'Chunking the challenge'

'Chunking the challenge' requires pupils to engage in processes and ask questions which appeal to very distinct styles of thinking. These styles will have been identified by using the IP3 tool.

Some people bristle at the 'Americanism' of the term *chunking* but it simply means doing what good teachers do all over the world – that is, ensuring that pupils know exactly what they have to do before they start their work.*

Chunking is also a very useful process for teachers/designers embarking for the first time on CSP in their classroom, since unclear patches in the design can be ironed out and pitfalls avoided in the future. CSP is a learning process which is always being refined,* since every class or learning community is different. It is dynamic, not a static package.

CHUNKING THE CHALLENGE
- one or series of images
- images must illustrate singer's experience
- bumper sticker or slogan
- singer's feelings about previous 10 years
- everyone involved in production and presenting

Given a limited amount of time – for example four minutes, since the use of such an unconventional time period alerts pupils to the fact that you *mean* four minutes – a sweep (page 38) can then be used to determine the view of the whole class on the details of the challenge. Once done and publicly displayed, pupils should be clear exactly what is to be done, in terms of content, roles and procedures.

* 'The shared criteria made it clear to everyone exactly what was expected of them.' (Forrest Howie, page 74: 'Assessment').

* 'Part of the high credibility of our programme is our willingness to acknowledge imperfection, reflect on it, and move on to try and do better next time.' (Bruce Bonney – see page 31).

Chunking also promotes 'whole brain learning'. By requiring pupils to focus their attention on the overall learning task and thereby see the big picture, it ensures that they regularly engage in 'right brain' operations. Then when they work systematically through the challenge to identify the separate elements, pupils are engaging in 'left brain' activity.

What the pupils do: B – 'Exhibit'

With a clear aim in mind, designers of challenges can construct focused activities which require pupils to demonstrate the knowledge, understanding and skills required by most school syllabuses. All challenges have within them specific, detailed criteria* which guide pupils in meeting the challenge:

* See the Academic Challenge, teacher version, on page 45.

➡ **rule criteria** – let pupils know the *processes* they must follow

➡ **content criteria** – define what their challenge must contain as a *subject* focus

➡ **form criteria** – define what the *product* must look like and sound like.

These criteria are clear from the beginning and are the *chunks* that the pupils must understand before proceeding. They constitute *quality criteria* against which success will be judged. They are *specific, observable outcomes.*

Throughout the challenge process pupils are expected to take responsibility for and ownership of their learning. And by using the various 'tools' that have been introduced to them, the process of collaboration and learning in an organised and thoughtful way is internalised. On completion of the challenge pupils publicly exhibit their learning.

What the pupils do: C – 'Debrief'

* Several of the vignettes indicate the value of the debrief phase for pupils. See, for example, Forrest Howie's subsection on 'Assessment' (page 74) and Brian Speedie's on 'The learning process' (page 98).

In the CSP model a great deal of importance is attached to the debriefing phase in which pupils have time to give and receive *feedback, review* their work and *reflect* on what they have done so that understanding is deepened.*

At first it may be difficult to get pupils to reflect at length or in depth on their work but once this process is embedded in the learning and teaching strategy it becomes a very powerful tool for consolidating learning. Debriefing does not only mean passing comment on the work of others. Sometimes it might involve journal or diary writing to answer the big questions such as:

'What do we do with this new learning?'
'What was the point of this learning experience/challenge?'

Asking pupils to reflect on what they have learned from a lesson or series of lessons is sometimes salutory, especially for the teacher who has just 'delivered' the lesson content!

Thought must also be given to the supportive nature of debriefing feedback. When it is part of a debrief or assessment structure, feedback is a conscious action and can easily be seen in operation. But what of the unintentional, negative feedback provided, say, when a conventional classroom based on assumptions of quantitative ability reminds pupils of their lowly place in the pecking order? Hence the importance of the supportive culture of the CSP classroom.*

* See, for example, the description of 'Ms. Fogg's' teaching approach in **Leading the Learning School** (pages 52–55)!

Self-assessment

Pupil journals and learning logs are tools designed to assist pupils in self-assessment. By allowing time for pupils to reflect on a period of work and comment on their thoughts and feelings as the work started, progressed and then reached completion, they encourage pupils to revisit the learning experiences in their memories. Learning is consolidated by setting pupils open-ended, reflective tasks. Understanding of the processes and outcomes – the learning targets – can then be monitored by regular teacher/coach feedback.

The feedback also performs an important function in that teachers are responding to genuine – maybe even negative – comments by pupils and that personal link is surely better than an arbitrary percentage mark written at the bottom of the page. Personal comment can inform pupils of their progress and ways forward.

Learning Log

Name: _Robbie_   Class: _____   Date: _3/10/02_

Please write your thoughts on at least 3 of the following questions

> What I learned was...
> What I found interesting about this work was...
> What surprised me was...
> I want to know more about...
> Right now I'm feeling...
> This experience might have been more valuable to me if...

1. What I learned was that people become very attached to what their working on, no matter what the subject or topic is and no matter how much they feel they cannot relate to their subject in the beginning.

2. What surprised me was people were willing to ~~attack~~ attack their friends over a 5-minute presentation.

3. Right now I'm feeling reflective, looking back on the events as a valuable learning experience.

The completion of the journal also encourages pupils to reflect in a coherent way on activities undertaken, which may otherwise only be understood in a flimsy way. Rather than being *told* that work done fits into a bigger picture, if pupils are encouraged to make connections for themselves that realisation will then be their own, and so a more solid understanding will emerge.

By articulating that understanding in a way that is, understandable by another person the learning process continues with the need to reflect, synthesise and articulate. This activity can also be two-way since, in a collaborative community, the views of pupils about the tasks, targets and outcomes are surely vital to the teacher/coach's own assessment of the effectiveness of an activity or strategy.

* See also in Brian Speedie's vignette: 'The learning process' (page 98).

Learning logs are usually more focused than journals. The example shown here asks pupils to comment honestly on their contribution within the group challenge.* The effectiveness of the log is dependent on the design of the self-assessment which, like challenges, can be reused and adapted to meet varying needs. The point is that once the hard work is done, it has a long shelf life.

Challenge – Self Assessment

Pupil Name   **Date:**

Challenge Title:
Group/Team Members:

Directions: Think about how much you contributed to the challenge just completed. Please respond to the statements below by circling the word which best describes your level of contribution. Please write some specific examples of your contributions that support your response.

1. On this project I shared my ideas, opinions and suggestions appropriately with the rest of the group.

rarely – sometimes – often – consistently

Describe at least one idea or suggestion which you shared -

4. On this project I helped the group to meet the standards of quality that went with this project.

rarely – sometimes – often – consistently

Describe at least one way that you helped the group meet the standards of quality that went with this project -

Leading EDGE LLC – Workshop Handout

The log is, naturally, underpinned by CSP theory and practices. Questions and directions are specifically aimed at reflection and review of recent or longer term performance. Pupils are also asked to justify their selection of behavioural options by describing specific, observable behaviours.

Peer assessment

Two CSP tools which assist this form of assessment are the *check-in* (see page 52) and the *huddle*.

The huddle is an opportunity for each group to get together and decide on a communal response. This response can take different forms. It can be a chance for groups to get together after a challenge and before a debrief, so that they can then check their perception of their own performance with the perceptions of other groups. They do this by asking themselves two key questions: *What went well? And what did not go so well?* This can also be an opportunity for teachers to draw their own conclusions about the effectiveness of their challenge design.

The huddle is also used after a presentation, when each of the groups in the 'audience' get together for, say, 30 seconds to agree on a united response to what they have witnessed. As a confidence building procedure comments should be directed only to the positive points of each presentation. However, as the groups become more confident in the process they can be encouraged to comment also on an area for improvement.

As a tool the huddle also provides a model for all participants in how – and why – criticism should and can be constructive. How often in classrooms have we seen the one voice comment – always from the teacher – and a passive response from the pupil who just 'grins and bears it'? What is gained by that? What interpersonal skill has been developed? No matter how apposite the teachers' comments, just how much of such criticism (both good and bad) is rejected simply because of its source?!

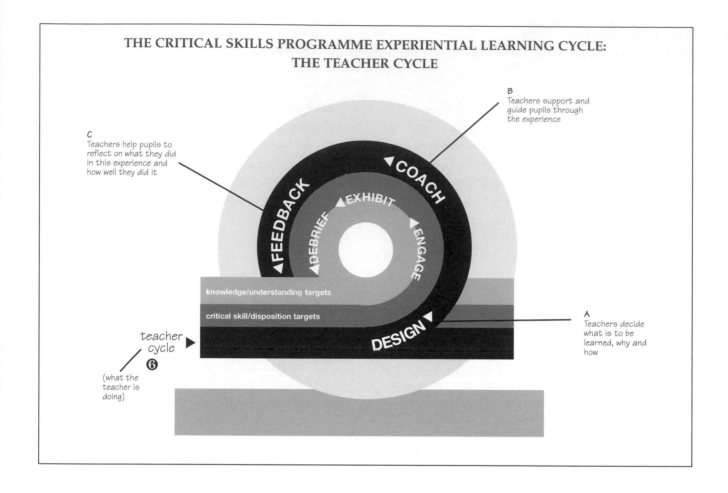

THE CRITICAL SKILLS PROGRAMME EXPERIENTIAL LEARNING CYCLE: THE TEACHER CYCLE

B
Teachers support and guide pupils through the experience

C
Teachers help pupils to reflect on what they did in this experience and how well they did it

FEEDBACK
COACH
DEBRIEF
EXHIBIT
ENGAGE
DESIGN

knowledge/understanding targets
critical skill/disposition targets

A
Teachers decide what is to be learned, why and how

teacher cycle ⑥

(what the teacher is doing)

6. The Teacher Cycle: What do teachers have to do?

The change in emphasis on learning style within CSP has major implications for the role of teachers. Rather than being the 'Great Provider',* teachers move to become designers, mediators, coaches and supporters within the learning process.

In other words teacher/coaches are *facilitators* – promoting effective learning through their own internalisation of CSP practices and ideas, including not only the careful design of integrated challenges but also the application of CSP ideas to their classroom management.

In any classroom at any time all pupils are paying attention to something – but to what? They may not *listen* to all you say but they will see what you do.* Therefore teacher/coaches have a responsibility to operate within the same CSP rules that they are asking their pupils to apply to themselves.

What the teacher does: A – Design

The importance of clarity in challenge design is crucial. Not only must pupils' tasks be clear and attainable but clear, observable *success criteria* must be built into them.

As will be seen, it is 'content' – however that is, defined – which generates the motive power within thoughtfully designed challenges. However, as will be shown later, a challenge should also be designed to help pupils develop social and organisational skills as well as knowledge and understanding of the content.

* See also Pete Fox's description of his 'Grand Lecturer' style! (page 69).

* 'Don't worry that your children don't listen to you. Worry that they are watching everything you do' (Robert Fulghum, quoted by Jack Drury in the **CSP Level 1 Training Manual**).

At first, the writing of challenges might seem fairly straightforward but when these are used in the classroom, teachers must be prepared to evaluate the clarity of each challenge in the light of pupil response.* If pupils have to ask what they have to do; why they are doing it; and/or how do they know if they're doing it correctly, then some redesigning is necessary!

* See also the comments at the end of the first paragraph on the huddle (page 57).

What the teacher does: B – Coach

The definition of a teacher as a person who gives pupils information and assesses how well they have learned their lessons is one that many people would accept. However, the CSP model encourages teachers to become *coaches* or *facilitators*, helping pupils to develop the abilities to achieve targets *on their own* and then realistically to assess their own performances.*

* See Forrest Howie's description of this role (page 74: 'Assessment').

Learning for understanding is seldom achieved through the delivery of self-contained blocks of information in response to closed questions. Rather, it is the performance of challenging, open-ended tasks that encourages the development of real understanding.*

* See, for example, the section on 'the learning process' in **Leading the Learning School** (pages 41–44).

Naturally, many pupils need encouragement to develop their skills, and some may want the reassurance and safety net of an answer to the 'how to' question. However, CSP practitioners try to avoid answering this kind of question, since any such response would limit the development of pupils who think and learn in different ways from their teacher. By unleashing the abilities and imagination of pupils, CSP is providing opportunities that they seldom get when they work to specific ends along more restricted routes.

However, the role of coach does not mean that teachers stand back and simply observe pupils working through various challenges with greater or lesser degrees of success. Teachers/coaches help their pupils to understand their learning tasks and in so doing promote self-esteem. They also encourage effective learning by generating high expectations and helping to develop collaborative relationships.

Raising self-esteem through CSP

> 'Have you ever tried to enthuse a pupil who has simply given up on school?'

Heather Swinson, 'A Special Needs Teacher's Experience', page 82*

* Heather Swinson's description of the construction and results of the 'Schoolopoly' game is required reading!

It is almost a truism that pupils reach as high as they are expected to. If teachers employ a simplistic model of ability which suggests that some pupils simply have lower levels and others higher, then not only do pupils quickly perceive the 'level' they have been allocated and respond accordingly but teachers can also reinforce these expectations.*

* See again the description of 'Ms. Fogg's' teaching approach in **Leading the Learning School** (pages 52–55).

How often do teachers 'talk down to', give much more simplistic, low-level tasks and generally reinforce the low self-esteem of these pupils? How often is difficult behaviour in the classroom really a distraction strategy used to disguise a pupil's fear of failing? If these questions are considered at the design phase important benefits can accrue: by raising confidence the reaction of pupils is more positive, promoting higher order thinking. And by providing the 'big picture' ('why are we doing this?') whole brain learning is also encouraged.

It is an almost impossible task to be aware of the emotional baggage carried by each individual pupil, but teachers and coaches are aware of the need to raise self-esteem, and a very effective way of doing this is to show that they have very real, high expectations for all their pupils.

Of course, in every school some pupils do have difficulties but CSP aims for inclusion.* By explicitly stating the high expectations for all pupils working through challenges, CSP pupils are encouraged to reach for higher achievement. Clearly, careful consideration must be given to the expectations and tasks set within a challenge and to the dynamics of the groups created. That is the challenge which faces the CSP teacher, as both challenge designer and coach.

* See, for example, the extract from the OfSTED report on Central Lancaster High's Year 11 Key Skills course in Linda Marshall's vignette (page 95).

What the teacher does: C – Feedback and Assessment

It was asserted earlier that CSP enhances assessment by providing new opportunities and a more instructive, formative system which encourages and informs pupils while also providing much fuller and individual reporting opportunities.

One of the first things that struck CSP practitioners when challenges were under way was the realisation that the conventional role of the teacher was redundant. To fill that vacuum teachers began to watch and listen more carefully and from that process evolved the idea of anecdotal evidence.

As pupils work, talk and interact, teacher/coaches can simply note what they see and hear. Since challenges are based on specific, observable criteria, checklists can be drawn up, comments added about group and individual performance, and teachers simply look to see whether those *process criteria* are being achieved.

Transforming Teaching & Learning

As an offshoot, discipline is also improved when pupils can be faced with their own words and actions when they are working – or not! – within the learning community. Rather than a teacher making a general complaint, a teacher/coach can ask a genuine question, feeding back their record of the pupil's own words and actions and asking whether or not they think they were responding appropriately within the class's agreed Full Value Contract. Finally, with clearly structured record sheets both pupils and teachers have 'hard copy' evidence to provide feedback, plan future steps, and engage in self and peer evaluation.*

* See the section on 'Use results to build a constituency for your approach' in Bruce Bonney's 'Advice for newly trained critical skills teachers' (page 124).

* See also the Academic Challenge, teacher version, on page 45.

In contrast to the anecdotal assessment tool which is aimed at process criteria, another tool – the *product quality checklist* – is used to assess the product of a group's work. Essentially, any challenge has as its product three elements:*

➡ **rule criteria** – have the rules been followed?

➡ **form criteria** – is the product structured in an appropriate way?

➡ **content criteria** – does the product contain detailed, relevant information?

PRODUCT QUALITY CHECKLIST

Date: _____

Product Author(s):	Product Title/Name "Whale Bulletin Board"	Evaluator Name(s):

(✔) Observed	Criteria	Possible Points	Rating
	"rule criteria" – Completed by Friday, 2.00 p.m.		
	"form criteria" – Informative – gives viewer important information about the subject		
	"content criteria" – Reveals connections among the physiology, behaviour and environment of whales		
	TOTAL		

Therefore the assessment structure is inbuilt to every challenge – the pupils know beforehand what they will be assessed on, and so a product quality checklist based around these three kinds of criteria is a fair, clear and easy way of assessing the product.

CSP opens up opportunities for several assessment strategies but has at its heart the belief that pupils must be aware, not only of the purpose of their learning, but also what they must do to achieve success. If a marksman cannot see his target is it surprising if he misses? Yet how often are pupils assessed when they are not clear what the criteria for success are or how to achieve them? CSP provides pupils not only with a destination focus but also the means of getting there.

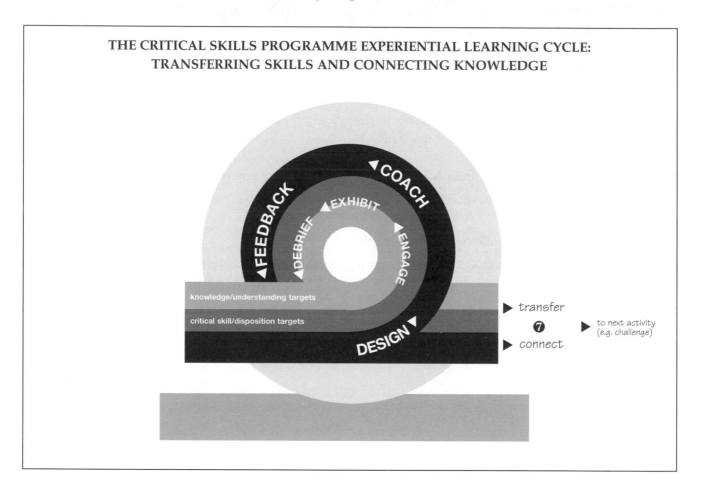

THE CRITICAL SKILLS PROGRAMME EXPERIENTIAL LEARNING CYCLE: TRANSFERRING SKILLS AND CONNECTING KNOWLEDGE

7. Transferring skills and connecting knowledge

The final part of the CSP cycle has now been reached but it is not an end in itself. Challenges do not have to be continuous but pupils do need to know why they have done them, how each connects to the 'big picture' of their learning, and have time to reflect and make connections for themselves. This is a difficult role for teacher/coaches who may be tempted to rush on to the next part of the course or the next challenge.

Having completed a challenge, are we sure that our pupils have made sense of it all? Are we, as teacher/coaches, reflecting on what pupils now know, what they understand, and what they can do, so that they can carry these qualities over, i.e. 'transfer' them into future learning experiences?

By providing time for reflection and connection-making, teacher/coaches are enhancing effective learning in other ways too. Has it become clear during the challenge process that certain skills need further attention? Is the learning community itself working or is it in need of some maintenance – even conflict resolution?*

* See Brian Speedie's description, 'The learning process' (page 98).

After this process of transfer and connecting has happened, pupils and teacher/coaches are ready to move on and the whole cycle can start again – but this time with sufficient tools and appropriate attitudes in place for the programme to become more than the sum of its parts, as everyone involved begins to internalise the processes and starts to use them to enhance learning in its widest possible sense.

> CSP, then, is not subject specific. Nor is it school specific. It is life specific!

Section Three: The Critical Skills Programme in Action

Ten Vignettes

CSP IN ACTION

Pete Fox – *English Teacher, Gilboa-Conesville School District, New York State, USA*

Introduction

Sometimes effective systemic change can begin with noble motivations, diligent research, careful planning and courageous actions. It can evolve with syntactical purity from the inspired rhetoric of those we look to for advice and direction. Then again, change can result from having our noses rubbed in the raw realities of school life.

While I would love to say that our experiences at Gilboa began with some carefully scripted plan for improvement, that simply was not the case for us. We changed because we were forced to confront school failure in many different facets of our operation. Somehow, in our retreat from pain, we found a path that saved us. And that is, the story I would like to tell here.

* 'Quality is a journey, not a destination' (J. M. Juran, a founder of the Total Quality Management movement).

To me, educational reform is not a 'programme' at all. It is a direction in which we travel.*   It is a vision framed by our beliefs, our aspirations and our ethics. I do not believe that there is any one path that leads to reform, and I distrust any 'authority' that says otherwise. I say this on the basis of my own experiences as a classroom teacher.

Gilboa-Conesville School

My school is the Gilboa-Conesville Central School in Gilboa, New York. It is a small rural school in the Northern Catskill Mountains about 120 miles north of New York City. We have about 400 students ranging in age from 5 to 18. At one time we were a thriving farm community, but economic conditions during the 1970s and 1980s destroyed most of our agricultural base.

Despite our economic woes, there was an enduring pride that held the school together. We had a stable community. Parents cared deeply about their children, and the school staff was committed to doing the best we could in rather trying times. Nevertheless, we struggled with high rates of unemployment, underemployment and poverty. While we had many successes in the school, we were not immune to the social problems that plagued virtually all other schools at the time. We were trying to cope with increases in student drug use, vandalism, truancy and misbehaviour. Our scores on state tests began to slip, and we slowly became a 'troubled' school.

At times it seemed hopeless because, despite our best efforts, we simply could not sustain the momentum we needed to create enduring reforms. We had trouble attracting good teachers and managers and there were frequent turnovers in our management team as successive headteachers simply used us as a stepping stone to jobs elsewhere.

By the early 1990s we were a school in crisis. In the spring of 1992 I was finishing my second decade as a high school English teacher in Gilboa. I had committed my entire career to the school, and, much as I loved the students and the community, Gilboa was a painful place for me to be.

At the time, I was a pretty successful classroom teacher. I had received a Teacher of Excellence award from the New York State English Council, and I was very active professionally. However, the drift in our school was depressing. By June, there was a particular act of vandalism that was the 'coup de grace' for me.

A student had spray painted an obscenity on a school vehicle on the night before the graduation ceremony for our seniors. For whatever reason, our school superintendent decided to have the truck parked for everyone to see during the ceremony. I remember sitting there looking at the truck and being overwhelmed by the sadness of it all.

It dawned on me that it was not simply a student problem. Somehow, we had all failed. After a twenty-year commitment to a cause I honestly believed in, I wanted to leave teaching and to do something else with my life. As I packed up my room for the summer vacation, I did so with the intention of using the time to explore a career switch. One of the great ironies of my life, however, is that, since I was not sure that I would be returning in the fall, I spent extra time putting my room in order before I left. This caused me to be one of the last teachers to turn in my keys.

As I was filling out the paperwork to receive my last pay-check of the year, my school principal, Matt Murray, happened to mention to me that he had paid for a training slot in a Critical Skills training program. He had not been able to get anyone else to attend it, and since I was the last person left, he asked me if I wanted to go. I quickly scanned the brochure, and noticed that it was being offered by the Antioch New England Graduate School in Keene, New Hampshire. I thought back to a great summer vacation that my family spent in Keene when I was 10 years old, and I accepted on purely selfish grounds. I figured that I might as well get a week's vacation from the school if I were going to leave. After twenty years, I deserved it.

To my chagrin, I later found out that I had not read the brochure carefully enough. The course, it turned out, was not being taught in Keene. Instead, it was going to be taught in a local school about three miles from my house. Instead of having a week's vacation, I had really only signed up for yet another in-service program. Cursing my own luck, I decided to fulfill the commitment I made, more out of a sense of grudging professionalism than from any desire to change my teaching practice.

Critical Skills training

I began the course with very little enthusiasm and even lower expectations. As we went through the activities on the first day, I grew increasingly uncomfortable with the experiential focus of the activities and with what I perceived to be a dismaying tendency to be far too 'touchy-feely' for my tastes.*

* In terms of the IP3 model (see page 48) Pete Fox is a very strong 'product' person. John Kerr (see pages 87–88) reports very similar feelings. John, too, is a strong 'product' person!

By lunchtime, I had decided to leave and even announced my intent in a large group session. I remember my exact words: 'I spent most of the late 60s and early 70s dropping courses that began this way, and I have no intention of staying here.' Bruce Bonney, who was teaching the course, spoke to me and asked me to at least stay for the afternoon session. Impressed by his sincerity, I acquiesced – and that decision saved my teaching career.

In hindsight, I know now that what made that particular day so painful for me was that it exposed all the inadequacies I had as a teacher. Until that moment, I thought of myself as being an excellent teacher. I was a highly competent stand-up lecturer who knew his subject content and who could deliver with all the authority of a Moses carrying the tablets down the mountain. I taught with passion, intensity and purpose. I did all that I was trained to do. The problem was that my training was inadequate to the needs of my students in the 1990s, and I learned that I had ignored some pretty fundamental issues in my classroom.

* See pages 36–43.

One of the first lessons that I learned during that institute was the importance of establishing a classroom community* and the impact that that community has on learning. I don't know why I had never made the connection before, but I recognized that what was slowly destroying our school was not that our students were stupid or that our teachers were incompetent. Our greatest impediment was our inability to create an environment to sustain our efforts at change.

Implementing Critical Skills

When I first went back to my classroom, I was not quite sure that I could teach my content in a new way, but I suspected that I could adapt the delivery system to address my curricular concerns. What I was not sure of was that I could change the culture of my classroom. In the early days of implementation, the hardest part for me was creating the climate for change. I worked very hard to establish a safe environment where people respected each other and worked to the best of their abilities. In Critical Skills terminology, we call this the *Full Value Contract** by which students (and teachers) work and play safe, fair and hard.

* See pages 41–43.

Fortunately, my efforts at implementing the model were supported in two important ways. First, my students were open to experimenting with a more experiential approach to learning.* When I initially laid out my intentions, one of my students said outright: 'Mr Fox, that is not you!' And he was right. It was not me, at that moment – but it was the me that I needed to become in order to continue teaching.

* As so many UK CSP trainees have found, pupils generally take to the experiential approach with great enthusiasm!

Transforming Teaching & Learning

The students helped me to learn to become comfortable with a process approach to teaching. I needed to give up some control and to abandon my role as the 'Grand Lecturer' in the class. I had to accept the fact that students would be more in control of their own learning. My role shifted a bit and my chief job was to find ways to convert my curriculum into problems that students could solve.* This began a process of discovery that has since become the norm in my class rather than the exception. It also helped a great deal that my wife, Jane,* was a primary teacher who, like so many primary teachers, had mastered the demands of a process classroom. Jane tutored me in my efforts and helped me adapt to a different style of teaching.

* See page 44.

* Both Jane and Pete are now lynchpins of the UK CSP training programme.

I cannot say that Critical Skills made teaching easier for me. Lecturing was easy for me, but it did not work for my students and it contributed to the nagging sense that I needed to do more in order to meet the needs of my students. What Critical Skills did was invigorate me and provide me with the motivation I needed to stay in teaching.* It changed my attitude toward my students, my classroom, my school and myself. I have had to work very hard to be a good Critical Skills teacher. There is no doubt about that. However, I have found this work to be the most rewarding time I have spent in teaching.

* This is a common refrain among CSP trainees. For example: 'CSP seems to rejuvenate teachers, brings back their old enthusiasms ...' (Ian Glen, Head of Schools, Midlothian); 'CSP has radically revitalised my enthusiasm for teaching' (Don Carlisle-Kitts, English teacher, Edinburgh).

Whole-school developments

At the end of my first year using the CSP model, other teachers in the school noticed how I had changed. They saw that I was happier and more enthusiastic about my job. My test scores on our mandated state tests improved (**Fig. 1** on page 70). My disciplinary referrals decreased dramatically (**Fig. 2** on page 70) and attendance rates in my classes increased significantly.

My students were enjoying class more and talking about the approach in other classes. It helped that I was a veteran teacher with an established reputation as a 'good' teacher. I had also served as our teacher union president and, for over twenty years, I was our union's chief contract negotiator. I am sure that, when my colleagues looked at me, they saw 'an old dog learning new tricks'.* Gradually, they went for Critical Skills training as well.

* See also John Kerr's observations in 'The teacher cycle' on page 34.

Our superintendent and principal gave us full support. They deliberately created a safe environment in which teachers were encouraged to take risks. They did not demand that everyone who went for training implement the CSP model. Instead, they encouraged all teachers to go for training and to implement whatever they felt was most appropriate for their personalities, their classrooms and their content areas. Most important, they themselves took the programme and began to conduct our staff

Gilboa-Conesville School:
percentage of students passing English examinations, 1988–2000

Figure 1

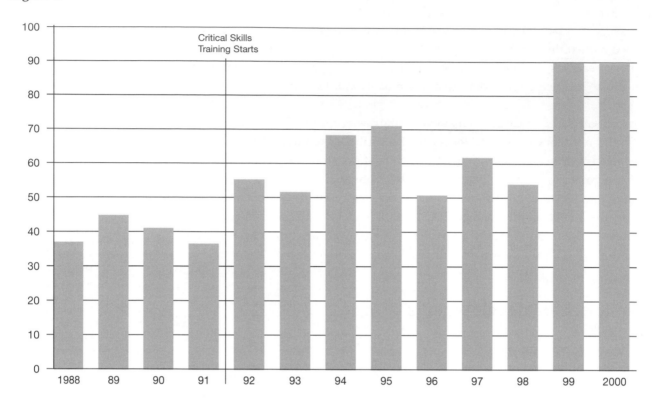

Gilboa-Conesville School:
discipline and vandalism 1991–1998

Figure 2

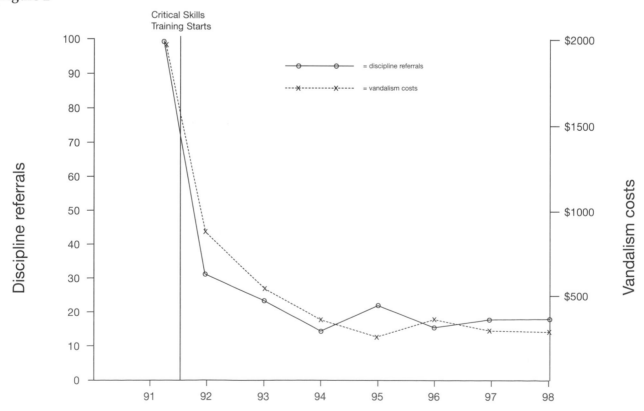

meetings in a CSP format. In essence, they helped establish among the staff the same kind of learning environment that the teachers tried to create in their classroom.*

It has been ten years now since Gilboa first became involved with Critical Skills. It is hard to distinguish between what is 'Critical Skills' and what is 'Gilboa'. I thought about this when I was in Edinburgh last spring with a group of Gilboa students and teachers who travelled there on our spring break.*

We met with some Scottish educators in the hotel where we were staying. They asked our students what they felt Critical Skills had done for them and how it had changed their attitudes toward school. The students could not really answer the question because they had been educated in a Critical Skills model since they were seven years old. For the most part, they knew no other system. What we had once struggled to implement had become the expected norm. I knew that morning in Edinburgh how thoroughly the Critical Skills Program can change a system. As our students struggled to find a polite answer for our guests, I knew we had arrived. We had changed the system!

'And the best thing – it works!'

* Anne Callan (page 101) describes how she used CSP tools to establish this kind of environment. See also Linda Marshall's comment that 'It is much easier to set up a collaborative community in your classroom if you already work in one!' (See 'Future plans for Critical Skills' pages 95–96.)

* This excursion was the outcome of a real life challenge (page 46) similar to one which features in the Level 1 training video.

Forrest Howie – *Senior Teacher, Sciennes Primary School, Edinburgh*

Introduction

To fully understand what Critical Skills has brought to my teaching it is necessary to look back to how I perceived many 'new' curriculum ideas before beginning my CSP training.

I had been teaching for four years, mainly in the upper stages of primary, and I felt fairly confident about what was expected of me and how I could best 'deliver' this in the classroom. Despite still being fairly new to teaching I was already becoming somewhat cynical about many of the new things coming out through in-service training.

To me, many of these seemed potentially beneficial but were let down in one or more of the following ways:

- ➡ they were poorly researched – there seemed to be little proof of their success with a variety of age ranges in a variety of schools
- ➡ they were inadequately funded – too much money was required to implement them in school
- ➡ they seemed to remove the autonomy and professional judgement of the class teacher.

I had experienced some in-service courses where I had left feeling enthused but also slightly frustrated. I felt that the theoretical strengths would be outweighed by the practical difficulties.

The training

When I started my CSP training I was interested in the programme but there was still a part of me which felt that it might not be as useful as it promised. In short, I was in a position where I needed to be convinced.

The CSP idea had to overcome my worries. I needed to come out from my training feeling that here was something I could use; something which would motivate my class; which would help meet the needs of the children, their parents and carers, as well as my own needs. It had to be workable, something which I could go in and use without expensive equipment or major reorganising of my timetable.

In the course of learning about CSP I realised that here was a method of teaching which *would* work. Here was something which would allow my pupils to work as teams and work towards learning and improving upon their *fundamental dispositions* and *critical skills*. These would improve attainment **and** do it in a manner which allowed me to use my professional judgement and skills. Of huge importance to me was the fact that CSP would motivate my class and do all this in a way which would bring my pupils together as a community.

Any new idea has to be realistic. An interesting aspect of CSP – which the trainers made perfectly clear – was that this way of teaching complemented rather than replaced more conventional methods. In other words, CSP is a development and not a revolution.* Importantly, it also meant that I could continue to use existing lessons without having to make huge changes or without having to completely rethink my way of using them.

* See Pete Fox's comments about 'old dogs and new tricks' on page 69.

Back in the classroom

The strengths of this style of teaching have become clear from my experience with it in the classroom. The 'proof of the pudding' would be how the children and their parents would take to it. A series of lessons with three very different P7* classes have unearthed some interesting points. I wanted to see my classes learning through doing something that they enjoyed and which would allow them to develop their skills.

* Primary 1–7 (P1–7) in Scotland is equivalent to Years 1–7 in England and Wales.

I was able to witness long periods of time – often up to 45 minutes – when every child in my class was 'on task'! This was something which occurred in all three classes, despite their very different compositions. It was brilliant to be in a class where I didn't need to address the whole group for some time once the initial teaching had been completed. This empowered the children – and it definitely empowered me!

I was able to cover most aspects of my 'forward plan' through a variety of CSP activities. This was yet another strength of the programme. There was a similar approach to each activity and yet there was a seemingly unlimited set of activities and products for the children to work on. This 'same but different' approach ensured continuity, progression and motivation for my pupils.

Designing and using challenges

One successful way of working was to give 'mixed ability' groups of pupils a challenge which consolidated a piece of written language work the class had been working on. For example, I would spend a number of class sessions teaching them how to write a newspaper report. The individual children would then each produce a draft piece of work. A short while later I would organise a challenge where the children would be asked to write a newspaper article as a group. Then they would be given a *scenario challenge** which saw them as a team of journalists working for a new daily newspaper. This challenge allowed them to use and consolidate their writing skills. The *product criteria* were taken straight from the relevant 5–14 test paper* marking grids. The work the children produced had to meet these criteria. Much emphasis was placed on this.

* See pages 46 and 50.

* See the subsection 'What the teacher does: C – Feedback and Assessment' on pages 60–62. The Scottish 5–14 tests are equivalent to SATS in England and Wales.

Careful structuring of groups saw each member achieve the maximum benefit from the lesson. Children with very different levels of language skill development benefited enormously from being able to discuss the criteria regularly with each other; and they were then able to produce a piece of work that would be used in the final product.

In the CSP training we had looked at the differing roles of the modern teacher. One school of thought saw them as the 'sage on the stage' while the other saw them as the 'guide on the side'. I soon found out that challenges had to be based on knowledge that the children had already been taught. They could develop, consolidate and extend their learning through challenges but they couldn't do this without having the initial knowledge given to them. A challenge wouldn't be successful if this groundwork hadn't been done.

* The 'transfer and connect' phase of the cycle (see page 62) provides a particular opportunity for 'good old-fashioned teaching' to provide the basic knowledge needed for a new topic or challenge.

This reliance on 'good old-fashioned teaching' was a clear example of the realistic approach the CSP model used. CSP teachers certainly have to learn a new set of 'guide on the side' skills; but there are still times when we also need to be the 'sage on the stage'.*

Carefully designed challenges also allowed me to use visual, auditory and kinaesthetic approaches to teaching. The groups' final product could involve one, or more, of these approaches.* This shows how the CSP model allows teachers to take on more recent knowledge of teaching and learning. Multiple intelligences work also complemented the challenges well.

* See the annotated academic challenge on page 45.

Assessment

I found that one real strength of CSP was the way I could assess my pupils. Paper assessment is one of the most used, most abused and most tiresome (for all concerned!) ways of checking on your pupils' progress. It has its place in school but I had always wanted to be more effective in my use of other types of assessment.

* See the subsection 'What the teacher does B: – Coach' on page 59.

* See the subsection on 'chunking the challenge', page 53.

CSP activities allowed me to spend most of my time assessing individuals and groups and I was able to offer help and suggestions at critical times in the lesson.* There were numerous natural opportunities for the children to use self and peer assessment and the shared critera made it clear to everyone exactly what was expected of them.* Assessment through the CSP approach became manageable, useful, clear and – dare I say it – fun! The children were quickly able to develop the feedback they gave into something that was more specific and positive. They also became better at taking on board constructive criticism.

Through the use of group challenges I was able to devote more time to preparation and less time to marking bits of paper. It is important to stress here that this 'free' time to assess, and the progression the children made, was solely down to the design of the challenge I was using. The importance of a worthwhile and well designed lesson is crucial and there were times when I realised that I had not planned challenges as well as I might have done. Continual assessment of my own performance, as well as what the children needed, was crucial to making full use of the CSP model.*

* 'Part of the high credibility of our programme is our willingness to acknowledge imperfection, reflect on it, and move on to try and do better next time. Modelling this attitude and pattern of behaviour is central to encouraging it in others' (Bruce Bonney, page 123).

Spreading the word

Parents and colleagues commented positively about work done by the class and some interesting stories about children enjoying the CSP lessons came to me. Group challenge news always seemed to filter home well and many parents were able to tell me quite a bit about what their children had done. I even heard tales of children volunteering to take work home so that they could have it ready for their group the next day.*

* Note how on-going CSP challenges provide a powerful way of making homework a valid, integral part of the learning experience rather than the 'add-on' chore that it so often is. Heather Swinson ('Daniel', page 85) reports a similar phenomenon in a very different educational environment.

Naturally, I was able to show how the children had developed certain skills through the challenges. The assessment opportunities also allowed me to use *anecdotal evidence* when discussing children at parents consultation meetings.

As a young teacher I felt enthused, empowered and revitalised. These feelings were in complete opposition to those I had had before the CSP training. Colleagues who had gone through the training with me said the same. The next step is to see how I can help to spread the word to other colleagues, as well as further my own training and experiences with CSP.

Audrey Gibson – *Assistant Principal Teacher of English, Cumnock Academy, Ayrshire*

Introduction

* The Scottish Standard Grade examination is equivalent to GCSE in England and Wales.

One of the most pressing issues for teachers today is how to foster in pupils a sense of personal investment in their learning. My colleagues and I wrestled with this problem during a meeting in the English Department. Close reading scores had been lower than expected in the Standard Grade* English 'prelim.' exam and we were searching for ideas.

Other than teach the skills thoroughly and model them in worked exemplars, what could we do? Were our pupils just lazy? We suspected that they hadn't even read the passage on which the questions were based. Armed with the wisdom we'd imparted to them, how could they have let themselves down so badly? Most frustrating, during feedback pupils had revealed that they were aware of how to do well in the test. Somehow, they'd absorbed the theory yet hadn't acted upon it.

Putting yourself in their shoes

* A set of 16 CSP posters, including 'STOP', is available from Network Educational Press.

Then it struck me – *The Tower of Power!* Recently I'd attended Part B of the CSP Level 1 training, in which I'd been introduced to the Standard Teachers Operating Procedure tool (STOP).* This is a step-by-step process that pupils can use to solve problems. The idea is that a format can be created which helps pupils to define and tackle any number of challenges in an organised and successful way.

Teachers attending the course had worked on creating STOP procedures and using them to solve challenges in small groups. Directly afterwards, we'd been issued a challenge by our co-ordinators in which, working as a large group, we had to build a tower to certain specifications.

Despite all our previous training, and our commitment to the usefulness of the STOP procedure, we failed to use it. Under pressure to complete the task in time, we ignored all we had learned about problem-solving and struggled through the task, failing to reach any consensus!

Wasn't this exactly what my pupils had done? They'd been taught how to tackle the exam, but under pressure they'd failed to put any of that knowledge to good use.

My Foundation/General* section was used to completing close reading test papers in class, according to my instructions. Absence, erratic behaviour and disaffection troubled the class. For some pupils, defying me was a way of asserting themselves. Thus, there were at least as many reasons not to follow the instructions and do badly as there were to do their best.

* There are three Standard Grade levels – Foundation, General, and Credit.

Providing opportunities for ownership

The CSP model encourages teachers to see opportunities for pupil ownership and develop accountability in pupils.* Our pupils had been given the information they needed to succeed, yet they were alarmingly disconnected from any responsibility for acting on it. So I decided to set my class the Challenge shown overleaf (**Fig. 1**).

* See the subsection 'Towards a Full Value Contract' on page 37.

I asked them 'How can we improve Standard Grade reading scores at Cumnock Academy?' and we then discussed the idea of a pupils' guide. The four focus questions covered the issues of preparation, what to do on the day of the exam, and the paper itself.

The class divided into three teams to address these questions. By setting the task in the form of a CSP *real life challenge*,* with concrete content, rule and form criteria,* pupils were made aware of the high standards I expected and of the potential usefulness of their finished product. I asked them to produce practical advice and information, presented in a user-friendly way and in a format that would be easy to photocopy.

*See page 46.

* See the subsection 'What the pupils do: B – "Exhibit"' on page 54.

Making pupils aware of the importance of the process was also essential if this challenge was to succeed. I'm sure most of us are tired of hearing the perennial question: 'Why do we have to do this?'* The involvement of the pupils from the early stages of the challenge helped make this transparent.

* See subsection 4: 'The meaningful context' on page 49.

I had explained that the challenge was a response to concerns that pupils were not doing their best in close reading, despite the strategies they had been taught in class. The pupils had agreed that, with final exams looming, 'I don't know why' really wasn't a satisfactory response. They saw the value in developing their knowledge of exam technique. The challenge was also a welcome break from doing past exam papers!

Figure 1. Close Reading: A Real Life Challenge

Close Reading Challenge

Question: How can we improve Standard Grade Close Reading grades at Cumnock Academy?

Challenge: Create a guide for pupils which will help them to be successful in the Standard Grade Close Reading exams. You should address the following questions:

1. *How should I prepare for the Close Reading exam?*
2. *What general information do I need to know about sitting the exam?*
3. *How should I tackle the paper and make use of time?*
4. *How will I deal with difficult questions?*

Focus question number four will be addressed by the whole class using past papers and a specially prepared workbook.

Information resources available to you:

➡ your teacher
➡ SQA exam timetable (advice, times, dates, rules, etc.)
➡ selected publications
➡ past papers.

Product criteria:

➡ *Content criteria:*
  ▪ Questions above will be addressed and good practical advice will be given.

➡ *Form criteria:*
  ▪ The guide is informative and easy to read.

➡ *Rule criteria:*
  ▪ The guide is easy to photocopy.
  ▪ It is produced by the agreed date.

Quality standards your teacher will be looking for:

➡ Problem-solving abilities: she will expect to see you brainstorming, distilling ideas and focusing on quality ideas.

➡ Knowledge of the course: she will expect to see you using your knowledge and extending it through reading and discussion so that you become confident in applying supportive strategies to your close reading preparation.

Achieving a culture change through problem-solving

As part of the challenge, pupils were required to use various problem-solving techniques such as *brainstorming, distilling* ideas* and focusing on quality. I hoped that they would gain confidence through reading about and discussing techniques for tackling the examination successfully. *See page 41.*

For these pupils, group work alone was something of a challenge! They did not mix well, so I had to begin the challenge very carefully: setting preliminary rules for group interaction, movement around the class and so on. Yet when I stepped back and left them to it, something magical occurred.

I saw pupils using a *sweep** of their group (a tool I'd recently introduced) to gather everyone's opinions. Two pupils in each group were acting as recorders, writing down all the responses with care. To my amazement, the boys I had feared would spoil the challenge for everyone were writing an additional question on the list I had given them. (See **Fig. 2** overleaf.) *See page 38.*

They were addressing the topic: *'What general information do I need to know about sitting the exam?'* Between *'What items should I bring with me?'* and *'How much time do I have?'* they had added: *'What do I do if I'm late?'* I had to sit down at this point as I felt rather dizzy!

The teacher as resource

A key objective of the challenge was that pupils would begin to identify and access the many resources available. The class itself was the primary resource. Another was the exam board's timetable, which gives advice and guidelines as well as the times and dates of the exams. I suspect that most pupils don't even look at the small print on this document, apart from the passages read to them at pre-exam assemblies.

Past papers were also available, as I'd set pupils the task of specifying how long it took to read the passages. Finally, as a veteran of exam preparation myself, I offered my services as a consultant and provider of publications which had helped me in the past.

As they worked through the questions, pupils divided up tasks which required research (such as the time it takes to read a paper – they got this horribly wrong!) and certain pupils took responsibility for these activities. Others suggested drawing up checklists of materials pupils should take into the exam. All of the above took one 55-minute period.

Stage two involved pupils examining study guides and the exam board timetable to fill any gaps in their knowledge. From my experience of sitting exams, they gained good anecdotal material which helped them recognise the validity of individual revision styles. This was reflected in the advice they gave to the imaginary worried pupil at whom their guide was aimed. This took about 25 minutes.

Pupils then proof-read and typed up their contributions. This was the most troublesome part. I had a very temperamental computer which let us down badly. It was a great pity because pupils were by now enthused: making notes in the margin and asking how to phrase their advice.

Figure 2: Results of the brainstorm/distillation activity

1. How should I prepare for the Close Reading exam?

➡ Is there anything I can do to prepare for this exam?

➡ When I am reading at home, what should I be paying attention to?

➡ Does what I eat influence the success of my studies?

➡ When should I start my revision?

➡ I often become stressed when I think of my revision. How can I overcome this?

➡ I tend to be very negative in my attitude towards exams. How can I change this?

➡ I become very bored when studying. I find it easy to give up and go out with my friends. How can I change this?

➡ Is there any advice you would give me for the night before the exam?

➡ Is there anyone who can help me?

2. What general information do I need to know about sitting the exam?

➡ How can I avoid panicking on the morning of the exam?

➡ What items should I bring with me?

➡ *What do I do if I'm late?*

➡ How much time do I have?

➡ How many reading papers do I sit?

➡ How do I know which to sit?

➡ When I get to the examination hall how will I know where to sit?

➡ What will be on the desk?

➡ Do I need to check anything before starting?

➡ What do I do if I:
  ● need a pencil?
  ● run out of paper?
  ● need to visit the toilet?
  ● feel ill?
  ● complete the paper early?

3. How should I tackle the paper and make use of time?

➡ How long does it take to read the Foundation paper?

➡ How long does it take to read the General paper?

➡ How should I tackle this?

➡ What will I do if there are words I don't understand in the passage?

➡ Is there anything in particular I should be thinking about as I read the passage?

➡ What do I need to remember about tackling the questions?

Fortunately, we were able to use some of the library computers. I would not normally have sent these pupils to the library unsupervised; yet on this occasion they came back with the job completed, and questions for me about graphics and effective fonts.

I was delighted with the results of their work. Had I thought of this challenge earlier, I could have made use of the school's well-equipped computer labs and we could have finished the project in the professional way we would have liked. However, the pupils all enjoyed the task ('This is the best thing we've done all year!') and I promised to 'publish' the guide for them after the summer break.

Reflection to cement learning*

* See the subsection 'What the pupils do: C – "Debrief"' on page 54.

In subsequent classes we covered more close reading past papers and pupils were able to discuss the value of the ideas they had generated. The discovery that their estimate of 4–6 minutes to read the paper was laughable, reinforced our discussions on how to read properly, anticipating questions that were likely to be asked. This, we agreed, was the ideal moment to revise the booklet.

Real world problem – real world product*

* See the definition of a real life challenge on page 47.

The challenge was a success. Pupils achieved high standards in content and form. In the process they learned to work co-operatively. They became 'experts' – something rare for a class at this level – sharing authorship of a valuable resource that I will use and develop with my new S4 class.*

* S4 in Scotland is equivalent to Year 11 in England and Wales.

This class was comprised of pupils who would not have bought a study guide, let alone read one; yet together they *wrote* one! Their exam results were excellent, despite the fact that they had been a very challenging class, and I'm sure that in part at least it was due to the 'can do' attitude that the Critical Skills Programme inspires.

'And the best thing – it works!'

Heather Swinson – *Learning Support Teacher, St David's RC High School, Dalkeith, Midlothian*

Introduction

Have you ever tried to enthuse a pupil who has simply given up on school? For many of us, this aspect of our work can cause the most heart searching. As a Learning Support teacher, I meet many pupils with a wide variety of educational, emotional and behavioural needs. Some of these pupils feel isolated from the wider school community. Their self-esteem is low and their enthusiasm for learning has waned.

Colleagues feel under pressure to provide for these pupils and may look to the Learning Support department for advice. Staff seem aware that in many ways the curriculum is not meeting the needs of all pupils. Frustrated by the churning out of work sheets for the 'able', 'average' and 'less able',* teachers desperately seek more appropriate ways in which to make teaching and learning more relevant to an increasing number of disaffected pupils.

* The 'Motorway Model of Differentiation'. See **Leading the Learning School**, page 38.

Background

I had never heard of the Critical Skills Programme before seeing an application form from our Education Department for the course, under the title 'Advanced Teaching Skills'. It almost slipped unnoticed among the pile of bumf on my desk. However, it aroused my curiosity and I signed up, hoping that the course would address some of the issues outlined above.

The course

I imagined that I would spend a sunny few days in June, cooped up in a hotel conference room, trying hard to concentrate as lecturers displayed a succession of indecipherable overheads on a distant screen. The reality was rather different. Like a disparate group of individuals cast away on a remote island, we found ourselves part of an educational community as we discussed issues, solved problems, made decisions, developed ideas, and so on.

There were no overheads. Instead, a bewildering range of multi-coloured charts fought for space on the walls. The titles were curious: 'Experiential Learning'; 'Chunk the Challenge', 'Carousel' to name but three. 'How on earth is all of this going to be relevant to teaching in Scotland?' I wondered.

Later we were to find ourselves caught up in a whirlwind, deluged by papers on theories such as Gardner's theory of multiple intelligences. Our skim-reading skills were challenged and our nerves frayed as group by group we were required to present our findings to the whole community.*

Exhausted after the efforts of the first day, I felt utterly dispirited. I seriously considered withdrawing from the course.* However, I persevered and slowly began to realise that so much of what was being said was relevant. By the end of the week I was hooked! I returned to school, hoping for an opportunity to put into practice some of what I had learned.

At the chalkface

The opportunity arose after the October mid-term break when one of our assistant headteachers let it be known that he was interested in studying the differences in learning styles between boys and girls. He was also interested in challenging 'able' pupils. Here was the opportunity I needed to pilot a CSP course.

The group I had in mind consisted of five boys – four from S3 and one from S5.* Most had some degree of impairment in motor skills. My head of department gave me her full support and the assistant headteacher asked me to pass on copies of my log to chart progress. This turned out to be an important tool for reflection and was particularly useful when HM Inspectors visited our school towards the end of the project.

The pupils

I knew three of the S3 pupils well, having provided in-class support for them in S1, followed by a course of occupational therapy in S2 to improve their motor skills. All had written language difficulties and one had ADHD to compound his difficulties. There had been behavioural problems caused by a poor relationship between two of the boys* in this group. The fourth S3 boy was dyslexic and had low self-esteem, while Scott, the S5 pupil, had motor, attention and perceptual difficulties and was liable to butt into conversations inappropriately.

Time allocation

Of the group's five periods of learning support, only two were allocated to the Critical Skills Programme, to enable specific support in other subject areas to continue. Each CSP session lasted for just over one hour and was mapped out in detail with a 'Plan of the Day' chart placed prominently for all to see. This proved especially effective in focusing attention and prevented wasting what time we had. The programme ran from the

* It is worth pointing out that Heather was among the very first UK teachers to complete Level 1 training, in June 2000. At that time we relied entirely on American readings and participants suffered a certain amount of 'information overload'. This has now been rectified!

* Pete Fox had a similar experience (see page 68). But as Pete himself says: 'Bruce Bonney, who was teaching the course ... asked me to at least stay for the afternoon session. Impressed by his sincerity, I acquiesced – and that decision saved my teaching career.'

* S1–S5 in Scotland are equivalent to Years 8–12 in England and Wales.

* Adam and Daniel – but see the subsection on Adam (page 85).

beginning of November 2000 until the end of May 2001, far longer than I originally envisaged.

Objectives

My main objectives in designing the challenge were not simply to encourage the pupils to gain a working knowledge of their school, but also to gain a greater understanding of their own special abilities as well as those of others. I hoped that by learning about terms such as *quality discussion* and *quality audience** their communication skills would improve. I wanted them to be able to present ideas to others clearly and effectively. I also hoped that they would learn to solve problems by *brainstorming* and *distilling* ideas, encouraging depth of thought. I also hoped to uncover some hidden strengths.

Creating the community

In order to create a small classroom community we went through all the procedures such as creating a team and devising the *Full Value Contract*, a process which took four weeks. The boys took the initial from each of their forenames and called themselves the 'MAD Js'.

They allocated tasks and I watched with interest as first Adam and then Mark was chosen as leader through the *thumb tool* process.* Jack had volunteered to become the leader but the others rejected the offer, opting to vote instead. I thought I ought to intervene but realised that I had to stand back to see what would happen.*

The challenge

I wanted to involve the boys in 'experiential learning' by designing a *real life challenge** which would hook them and sustain their interest over a period of time. This was it:

In St David's, first-year pupils find it difficult to find their way around school. Design a board game which would enable them to become familiar with the layout.

The response was great. 'I'm up for it!' declared Jack.

Through a process of brainstorming they decided to call the game 'Schoolopoly'. As they designed the board, pieces, tokens and cards, other pupils in the department watched with increasing anticipation, keen to see the final product. They even haggled over how much they would be prepared to pay for the game should it be manufactured!

---

* See the subsection 'Towards a Full Value Contract' on pages 37–43. Rick Lee (see page 106) describes these as 'probably the two most effective tools... which we adopted'. Many CSP trainees would agree with this observation.

* See page 39.

* Many other 'novice' CSP teachers have reported going through a similar experience – and then finding that the pupils usually managed to work things out for themselves. True 'student-centred learning'!

* See the definition of a real life challenge in Section 2 (page 47).

Impact on individual development

→ **Mark**, who was not a natural leader, took on the role with good humour. His moment of glory came during the visit from HM Inspector when he took part in a presentation for the first time, having chaired the meeting with great aplomb. Through time, I realised that the self-esteem of this reluctant leader was rocketing! It was one of many positive surprises which arose from the programme. It was of vital importance to Mark that there was an end product* to give meaning to all the brainstorming and decision-making. He wanted so much to have a copy of the game for himself.

* Mark is clearly a 'product' person! (See the description of the IP3 tool on page 48.)

→ **Daniel**, who was responsible for the graphic design, created badges for the MAD Js and many of the items for the game. His self-esteem improved enormously as he realised the importance of his role within the group. He showed that he was highly motivated by being willing to continue with the work at home.* He was the first to volunteer to take part in a presentation to the AHT, and then later, to the Inspector.

* Forrest Howie (see page 75) also notes how on-going CSP challenges provide a powerful way of making homework a valid, integral part of the learning experience rather than the 'add-on' chore that it so often is.

→ **Adam**'s role as timekeeper was initially ironical. He would turn up late until the group brainstormed and decided that latecomers would have to make tea for the others! He would also go off on tangents until his comments were written on 'Post-it' notes and consigned to *the bin*'!* This was an instant cure. It wasn't long before members of staff were beginning to notice change for the better. Group members noticed it too. During a *debrief* session* Mark commented: 'I didn't know Adam could work so hard!' Daniel and Adam had had a poor relationship, but it improved to such an extent that Daniel was able to say of Adam's contribution to the presentation to the Inspector: 'That was better than mine!'

* i.e. Comments Box. See John Kerr's description of how to use this tool (page 90).

* See page 54.

→ **Scott**'s role was vital as the group's recorder. His relatively proficient writing freed the boys to develop their verbal communication skills. Although he was older than the others he fitted in well and made a positive contribution to the group discussions. He managed to control some of his more inappropriate interruptions, a trait which had previously caused exasperation among staff and pupils alike.

→ **Jack** left to go to another school a few weeks into the project. This was a pity, as there were real signs that he was beginning to benefit as the others undoubtedly did.

Conclusion

I am now in no doubt as to the value of this programme. The pupils were highly motivated throughout. *Check-in* time* at the beginning of every session gave each pupil insight into the interests and emotions of the others and in so doing deepened relationships. It was a great adventure, full of surprises. The boys have learned to persevere when faced with problems. They have learned that stumbling stones can become stepping stones.

*See page 52.

* Many other teachers have made similar comments. Anne Callan (see page 101) is now basing her school's Personal and Social Development programme entirely on CSP.

I agree wholeheartedly with the Inspector, who noted that this programme could be considered as part of an early intervention scheme. Although I did not target self-esteem and behaviour at the outset, these were areas in which remarkable progress was made.*

The programme has created its own momentum. Staff involvement has been crucial in encouraging the boys. The MAD Js asked if they could show their English teacher and classmates what they had been doing. For the first time they were involved in a presentation to their peers.

Their classmates gave them their undivided attention. My colleague, full of enthusiasm after witnessing a CSP session, began to talk enthusiastically about developing group discussion and solo talks which would fit well with the English curriculum. We speculated about the fun we could have developing various projects, but we soon realized that finding time would be the largest problem.*

* This is one important reason why it is essential that school senior management understand and commit to the CSP model.

When the class was dismissed, two classmates lingered behind. They wanted to play the game. One has many behavioural problems; the other, low self-esteem...

'And the best thing – it works!'

John Kerr – *Head of History, Balerno Community High School, Edinburgh*

Introduction

On a spring day in 1999 I attended a seminar in Edinburgh advertised as an introduction to a way of enhancing classroom learning. It was called 'Education by Design'.* and it seemed like a grand day out.

When I arrived I saw an eclectic bunch of people and was surprised by the number of education managers present from many areas of Scotland, and from primary, secondary and tertiary education*

The experience began with a short talk from Pete Fox who certainly seemed to be the 'real thing' – a classroom teacher who spoke as he felt and looked as though he could have made a successful career as a New York cop! Quickly he moved on and started our transformation into disciples.

The initial 'CSP' experiences came thick and fast. To 'socialise' us we made contact with our fellow group members by making animal noises! We then had to share ideas and present them to the assembled groups. We were given acronyms such as WASH ('We All Speak Here') to deal with, and *carousels** to make us think and walk at the same time – unheard of at most in-service courses.

* 'Critical Skills' was renamed 'Education by Design' in the USA in the mid-1990s. We have reverted to its original title for UK use because of potential confusion over the abbreviation 'EBD'!

* This seminar was originally planned for 20–30 people. In the event it attracted over 80 and became the starting point of CSP in the UK.

* See page 41.

* See page 53.

* See page 68.

We then had the Americanese of *chunking the challenge** to cope with. All in all, being then a classroom teacher of 26 years experience, I thought I'd had enough. 'All too 'airy-fairy' and 'touchy-feely' for me,' I thought. And then I listened to Pete tell a similar story about his own first reaction to CSP.* 'Stick around till after lunch,' he advised. I did, and went back for more!

Level 1 training

After this initial taster day many of the Edinburgh teachers were so enthused that they established after-school sessions linking some of the CSP principles with other work on brain-based learning. And then finally, in February 2000, came our first full Level 1 training experience.

* See page 33.

The experiences of Level 1 training are many and varied. We were put immediately into the *experiential cycle** and I saw in myself reactions I observe frequently in my pupils, ranging from initial wariness, even resistance, to uncertainty – just wanting to 'get on with it' – and then the realisation that as our ideas collided, fused and gelled, many worthwhile educational goals were being achieved and reinforced.

* 'Education is not the filling of a pail but the lighting of a fire.' (W. B. Yeats)

The important thing that I took from all the training days was the feeling that a spark was being lit,* or even rekindled, which made me think about the delivery of lessons and the experiences of the learners. But, most important, it provided me with the means and encouragement to stand back and think about what I was doing. Conceited as this may sound, I felt that I was already a very good classroom teacher. What the CSP trainers did was to open up the possibility of being better!

Back in school

*See page 44.

As I designed and put *challenges** into practice, it became more and more clear that individual challenges are in fact vehicles that carry much more than the subject specific content. Given the focus that has emerged recently on citizenship issues, for example, the *collaborative community** engendered by CSP has much to offer. The most obvious result of moving towards what was then a very elementary 'CSP classroom' was the very positive reaction of the pupils. I have found that such challenges incorporated into a programme of learning are stimulating, informative and rewarding for both teacher and pupils.

* See pages 36–43. Many people have observed that, while CSP challenges are a powerful way of enabling pupils to develop subject knowledge and understanding, the emphasis on developing such a collaborative learning community is an equally powerful way of promoting pupils' personal and social development.

Criticisms of such a programme of challenges, experiential learning and debriefing have often centred on the question of time. I have found that the positive benefits far outweigh these concerns, but to be realistic, yes, a bare minimum practical timescale for a challenge is three 40-minute periods. And on larger, more detailed challenges, at least four periods are required. But perhaps the following example will give some idea of the scope and breadth that challenges can offer to external examination candidates.

With a senior 'Higher' class of 17 year olds the topic was the US slump of the early 1930s, which they had studied conventionally for a short time. Having issued them with the words of the song 'Buddy, can you spare a dime', I then gave them the following challenge (**Fig. 1**).

Figure 1: An Academic Challenge*

Topic context: The USA 1920–32 – Boom or Bust

Your challenge:

- ➡ Work in groups of 4 or 5.
- ➡ Having read the lyric and listened to the song 'Buddy can you spare a dime', then watched the video, your task is to produce one large image or series of images illustrating the experience of the singer of the song.
- ➡ Design a bumper sticker or slogan capturing his feelings in 1932 (when the video was set), looking back over the previous 10 years.

Rules:

- ➡ Everyone participates in the production and presentation.
- ➡ Work within the given time scales.
- ➡ Meet the product criteria.

Time scales:

- ➡ grouping, reading and planning – 30 minutes
- ➡ designing and production ready for presentation – 30 minutes
- ➡ presentation, debriefing – 50 minutes

So the challenge for the pupils was to draw images and invent a slogan, all of which would capture the feelings of the singer of the song as he saw his life change from a builder and defender of the American Dream to one who saw no future.

* For a definition of an academic challenge see page 46.

Clearly, relevant factual content was a central part of this exercise, but learning strategies were also present in the planning. Transference of learning; the internalisation of information from one medium into another; the use of different senses and therefore brain stimuli; empathy; visualisation of concepts; reinforcement of learning; and the need to supply appropriate and accurate information during the *debrief**, were all carried forward by this one challenge.

* See pages 54–57.

Reflection is an integral part of the experiential cycle and it is crucially important for the teacher, too, to review the work done since pupils who are given some independence may well take unexpected – and possibly unwelcome – routes. For example, in constructing a challenge on US civil rights campaigns I asked pupils to adopt the roles of a segregationist or an integrator. When two groups adopted the segregationist stance I was left with the feeling that some pupils were using the exercise for what could be construed as a racist agenda. Time for reflection and refinement!

CSP and discipline

* See Heather Swinson's comments at the top of page 86.

A key point made by our trainers was the spin-off of implications for *discipline*.*

* See 'Towards a Full Value Contract' on pages 37–40. See also Rick Lee's comments on page 106.

By introducing a degree of prior agreement about class behaviour (the *quality audience*)* all pupils have their say about the class code of conduct. I have found this a very useful tool when talking to pupils who find it difficult to sustain membership of the disciplined group they agreed to be in. The opportunity for dialogue in which the pupils can reflect on their behaviour within the boundaries of their agreement is a very subtle but effective pressure on them.

Reporting and assessment

* See 'What the teacher does: C – Feedback and Assessment', page 60. See also Forrest Howie's comments about the value of this process ('Assessment', page 74).

I was intrigued by the idea of 'anecdotal assessment evidence'.* Essentially it means gathering notes and observations while pupils are on task and the teacher is no longer the direct provider of the learning experience.

As soon as I started experimenting with this way of making, admittedly subjective, comments I was very quickly able to compile extensive individual comments about all members of the class. Another feature was that the comments dealt with aspects of pupil activity which are not easily assessed within more formal assessment procedures. Organisers, 'drones', verbal and non-verbal communicators, co-operative and not so co-operative pupils, social types and independent workers – they all advertise themselves when teachers have time to observe their differing modes of learning in action.

On a less academic level, just seeing pupils in a different classroom dynamic added to – and sometimes changed – my perceptions of the class as individuals. A vital part of any challenge is that all pupils participate in the production and presentation of their work. Sometimes a few pupils – often those most in need of social skill development – are reluctant to take part in the presentation, but almost always they can work this out within their group and negotiate ways of meeting the criteria without being teacher directed.

'In the bin'

* i.e. Comments Box. Heather Swinson also describes using this tool to good effect in a rather different situation! (See 'Adam', page 85.)

Another useful tool introduced to me by CSP has been *the bin** – in my case a bright blue plastic bin. How often in class are we aware of pupils who have questions to ask but not the confidence to 'go public'? By having a place in the classroom where pupils can post anonymous notes with observations, requests or questions I can easily detect insecurities and/or misunderstandings and use this 'feedback' as starting points for the next lesson.

Silver linings and clouds

Despite a universally enthusiastic reception by those of us who have undertaken the training, it is all too easy for managers to see the 'wrapping not the product' and believe that a limited amount of training in CSP techniques makes us into seasoned practitioners, able to train our colleagues effectively. I am assured that this situation happens regularly in the USA – 'CSP on the cheap' – and two of my own experiences suggest that the same thing could all too easily happen here.

The first of these was in a city-wide in-service where a colleague and myself were allocated less than an hour to deliver 'the CSP experience'. We started each session with a very brief piece of theory and context-setting, then implemented a challenge designed to create a cohesive community. The result was very positive, but without adequate time to make clear the underlying philosophy we were left with the feeling that senior managers saw CSP only as an interesting novelty. As one participant later said: 'I liked it but I already know how to draw a poster.' Point – and opportunity – missed.

A more successful outing was with a group of probationer teachers who arrived expecting a conventional talk. In the next 90 minutes they had become a cohesive, *collaborative community** and had radically changed the shape and dynamic of the room. In that time all the things that one would hope to achieve over time in a classroom were present – colour, humour, assessment, structure, talking, listening, production, reflection and decision-making.

* Several headteachers and other senior managers – e.g. Anne Callan (page 101) – have reported that CSP tools are particularly effective in generating a collaborative ethos among staff.

The reaction from this reservoir of new teachers was extremely enthusiastic. But unless there is sustained support and encouragement CSP will struggle to survive in a few enclaves peopled by 'lone rangers'. Local authorities must be prepared to finance the full package of training and support. Without that, glimmers and hints of CSP will crop up in assorted in-service programmes for a while, then fade. Even the committed have to be inspired, refreshed and encouraged.*

* Bruce Bonney develops this theme further in 'Staying Alive with CSP' (page 121).

'And the best thing – it works!'

Vignette 6: A Secondary Whole-School Perspective

Linda Marshall – *Assistant Headteacher, Central Lancaster High School*

Introduction

As an Assistant Headteacher I have particular responsibility for developing teaching and learning in the school. I have been interested in putting new theories about how children learn into practice throughout my teaching career, and have used my own teaching experience in RE to experiment with the various learning theories which have been developed during my twenty years in schools.

It was through this interest in teaching and learning that I became involved with the work of Network Educational Press. Their conferences on differentiation, followed in recent years by their publications on effective teaching and learning, have given fresh impetus and enthusiasm to my own teaching. It was with great intrigue, therefore, that I embarked on the Level 1 CSP training in Edinburgh in October 2000 and February 2001.*

My experience of the CSP training

I have been fortunate to receive a fair amount of high-quality in-service training throughout my career. However, I certainly did not expect to receive such inspirational training as the CSP Level 1 proved to be. Usually, the desire to implement new ideas into one's professional practice subsides with the reality of school life and demands, and although one leaves such courses determined to make changes in the classroom, it is easier to revert back to 'familiar' styles of working.*

The Critical Skills Programme was like receiving the 'picture on the lid of the jigsaw' that I have been trying to complete for years. All the theories about pupil learning, teaching methodology, learning styles, assessment and pupil motivation could suddenly be 'fitted' into a structure which made sense. The training itself was one of the most intellectually and professionally challenging experiences I have ever been involved in, both as a student and as a teacher. The *collaborative community** which was set up by the highly trained and inspirational American trainers was the key to the success of the

* The six days of Level 1 training is generally divided 3 + 3 in the UK, though in the USA – where training is usually undertaken in the summer vacation – it is generally 5 + 1.

* This phenomenon has been described as the 'bunjee rope syndrome'! (See **Leading the Learning School**, page 10.)

* See pages 36–43.

institute. The training proved to be my professional 'road to Damascus' experience – not bad for an RE teacher, even if it was Edinburgh rather than Damascus!

The experiential approach adopted throughout the training helped to develop a collaborative community among the teachers involved. It was refreshing to work with colleagues from Scotland, who gave a fresh insight into teaching. The institute was challenging, hard work, but most important, it was great fun.

The trainers explained how they used the CSP model in their own classrooms, which gave currency to all the institute participants. The concerns that had led American teachers to develop the CSP model* matched the concerns of UK teachers and I was able to see how the model could be applied in my own classroom and, eventually, the whole-school.

* See page 32 – 'How CSP began'.

Putting CSP theory into practice

Following the training I couldn't wait to put the theories into practice in my own classroom. The head of RE and I have now developed a large number of challenges for use with pupils in Years 7, 9, 10 and 11. While we are still relative novices in using the CSP model, we can already see changes in how pupils learn and the atmosphere created in the CSP classroom. The enthusiasm of the pupils is very encouraging, and for the first time in my teaching career I can't wait for the new academic year to start so that I can set up collaborative communities in all my classes.*

* This 'can't wait' comment is a widespread response to the Level 1 training.

The RE department at Central Lancaster High School has long been an advocate for supported self-study and has used study guides to implement the requirements of the Locally Agreed Syllabus for RE. Writing *challenges*,* therefore, was not a difficult task since we were used to this style of working. Challenges we have written include 'The Christian Community' (Year 7), 'The Holocaust' (Year 7), 'Sikh worship' (Year 7), 'Non-violence – Martin Luther King' (Year 9), 'Prayer in Islam and Christianity' (Year 10), 'Christian and Muslim Worship' (Year 11 GCSE).

* See page 44.

We have used the CSP *toolkit** to support our work and have been particularly impressed with the quality of *peer assessment*.* For example, when Year 7 completed the challenge on the Holocaust, each group was given a 'Post-it' note on which to write positive comments on other groups' work and to suggest ways in which it could be improved. This form of assessment helped pupils to set targets to improve their work in the next challenge. The effect of this formative assessment on the quality of their work was very positive.

* See 'Towards a Full Value Contract' (pages 37–40).

* See 'Peer Assessment' (page 57).

In writing challenges we have achieved the following:

- ➡ We have provided pupils with a structure which enables them to cover the *knowledge and understanding* necessary in the RE syllabus.

- ➡ We have given pupils flexibility to use their preferred *learning styles*.

- ➡ We have encouraged pupils to *work collaboratively* with others.

- ➡ We have offered opportunities for pupils to *reflect* on their learning and to set *personal targets* to improve.

- ➡ We have given pupils *encouragement and praise*, both from the teacher and from their peers.

- ➡ Pupils have felt *challenged and enthusiastic* towards their work.

- ➡ The teachers involved have found it a fresh and exciting way of working which enhances their *professional development* as well as their *personal motivation*.

Some problems – and solutions

However, implementing Critical Skills is not without problems. The three main ones that we have encountered are highlighted below, together with suggestions about how they might be solved.

- ➡ **Problem 1** – In the RE department we only have one lesson per week. Setting up a collaborative community takes valuable lesson time and since this is the key to CSP, pressure of getting through the syllabus might lead to abandonment of the programme.

- ➡ *Solution* – We worked with the drama department to maximise curriculum time, using drama techniques to set up the collaborative community. Working with colleagues in other departments also helps to shift CSP into the whole-school, reinforcing the message with pupils, and enabling good practice to be shared. Our experience with the model has already shown that time invested in setting up a sound collaborative community leads to time being saved later on. Our Year 7 pupils are now working much faster than they did at the beginning of the year.

This success is borne out by an OfSTED report on the RE department in October 2001 which included the following comments:

> '...standards in lessons seen were above ... expectations. This is due to the introduction of Critical Skills strategies ... These improvements are gradually making a difference throughout the rest of the school. The quality of teaching and learning was never less than good in any lesson seen and they are very good overall. Consequently, pupils' attitudes and behaviours are also very good.'

- ➡ **Problem 2** – It has been more difficult to implement the model with older pupils – particularly in the middle of the year when their 'community' had already been well established! As a result, some of the challenges with older pupils have been less successful, particularly with already disaffected pupils.

➡ *Solution* – It will be much easier to set up this style of working with younger pupils at the beginning of the academic year. However, there is scope for using the model with the more established pupils; but they must have a sense of ownership so that using the peer group is more effective.

This success in applying the model with older pupils is witnessed in this extract from the above-mentioned OfSTED report:

> 'Key Skills courses are provided for lower attaining pupils or disaffected pupils... This is very good provision ... pupils are very much encouraged to organise themselves and take responsibility for their own learning ... Pupils took the lead of the lesson when making a co-operative presentation. They became very effective peer educators themselves. This was a teaching and learning partnership of the highest order and showed the real impact of the school's (Critical Skills) approach to social inclusion.'

➡ **Problem 3** 'Initiative overload' may mean that teachers are less willing to take on board yet another way of working.

➡ *Solution* – The ideal solution would be for the whole staff to be involved in CSP training. However, since most schools will be unable to do this it is important to choose carefully the staff who might be interested and then able to influence their peers.*

* In 'Advice for Senior Managers' ('Select healthy plants', page 132) Bruce Bonney discusses this issue in some depth.

Critical Skills pulls all the current national initiatives together, and is also professionally rewarding. For example, the implementation of key skills can be easily done through challenges.* Our RE challenges contained a key skill which both teacher and pupils assessed by means of evidence collected in the pupils' work, self- and peer assessment. This makes life easier for the teacher, not harder.

* See, for example, the OfSTED comments above.

Future plans for Critical Skills at Central Lancaster High School

I have already shared my experiences with my Head of Department, who has herself now undergone Level 1 training. We intend to introduce the new GCSE syllabus for RE as an entire Critical Skills challenge. We believe that this will give us an ideal opportunity to continue to raise standards in RE.

However, in my role as Assistant Headteacher with responsibility for teaching and learning, I am also eager to adopt a whole-school approach. In order to achieve this it will be necessary to take the following steps:

1. The initiative needs to have the full support of senior managers (including the Governors). Without their support, understanding and vision, the programme will remain isolated in individual classrooms.*

* See Bruce Bonney's comments ('Seek out friends and allies', page 123).

2.   Teachers need to see that it works before they embark on yet another initiative. This involves sharing good practice, with teachers observing lessons where the model is being used. Performance management objectives and school monitoring and evaluation cycles might provide a forum for such professional development to take place.

3.   When sufficient teachers have been trained to Level 1 it may then be time to introduce the programme to the whole staff. The best advocates for such change are the pupils themselves. They may demand change in their classrooms if they see a style of working which suits them and raises standards.*

* Many Critical Skills teachers report that, once given a challenge, pupils demand more.

4.   Teachers themselves need to work in a collaborative community, where they have time to reflect on their professional practice. Time must be found for this if CSP is to be successfully implemented. It is much easier to set up a collaborative community in your classroom if you already work in one!*

* Several headteachers have reported that CSP tools are particularly effective in generating a collaborative ethos among staff. (See for example page 101).

From my experience in implementing the model I believe that Critical Skills enables teachers to achieve the characteristics of effective teaching described by Hay McBer's *Research into Teacher Effectiveness* (DfEE June 2000). An observer of a CSP lesson, for example, would undoubtedly see evidence of the following:

> 'All teachers demonstrate a passion for learning by providing a stimulating classroom environment, giving demonstrations, checking understanding and providing whole class, group and individual practice in using and applying skills and knowledge. They constantly differentiate teaching and learning when it is appropriate to do so, to help all pupils to learn and to tailor opportunities to practise, embed and extend new learning to each pupil. Outstanding teachers are able to go further in the extent to which they are consistently able to support all pupils in their classes to think for themselves, and to deepen their understanding of a subject or skill.'*

* The OfSTED comments already quoted clearly indicate that this is happening in Lancaster Central High School!

Brian Speedie – *Senior Teacher, Bruntsfield Primary School, Edinburgh*

Introduction

I wasn't too sure what to expect when I turned up for the first morning of Critical Skills training. I'd attended courses on accelerated learning, thinking skills and learning styles fairly recently, and I had a vague notion that Critical Skills would connect with these in some way.

What I didn't anticipate was the profound influence that Critical Skills was to have on my own approach to teaching and learning. My experience was to be of a course which brought together many of the (often all too disparate) ideas I'd become interested in, but which I'd found difficult to integrate into my teaching on a daily basis. Critical Skills provided a framework and methodology which was to become of immediate practical use.*

* Linda Marshall makes a very similar comment. See 'My experience of the CSP training' (page 92).

At the time of my Level 1 training Forrest Howie and I were colleagues at Bruntsfield. It is enough to say here, therefore, that my thoughts and experiences echo his. Like Forrest, I've developed team challenges* in a number of areas of the curriculum, and I have no doubt that all pupils have benefited significantly from the CSP approach in a number of ways.

* See page 52.

Children working together

The group of 30 Primary 7* children I currently teach have many strengths, but it was abundantly clear at the beginning of the year that 'working together' wasn't one of them!

* Primary 1–7 (P1–7) in Scotland is equivalent to Years 1–7 in England and Wales.

A small number of individuals appeared to dominate group work, and there was a tendency towards organisational chaos after relatively short periods of time. My CSP training, therefore, was timely, to say the least: It allowed me to develop the principles of effective teamwork with my class. Pupils are now much more aware than they were of the importance of sharing responsibility; of finding ways to communicate effectively with their peers; and of involving *all* team members in the decision-making process.

Setting goals

* See, for example, the annotated Academic Challenge (Teacher Version), on page 45.

* See the annotated Academic Challenge (Pupil Version), on page 45.

I believe that giving children the 'Big Picture', as well as the detailed *success criteria** by which their work will eventually be judged, has helped to raise the levels of attainment of all pupils in my class. Children have been involved in evaluating their own work, and assessing the work of other groups. They have also been given the freedom to work towards clearly defined goals in their own ways, allowing for different *learning styles.**

The learning process

Pupils have presented their work to other teams on a regular basis, and they have received feedback from other children. Through first-hand experience, they have learned to appreciate that criticism is only likely to be constructive in an atmosphere of mutual trust and respect, and that strengths must be highlighted before any shortcomings may be addressed.

* See 'The check-in' on page 52).

* See 'Self-assessment' on page 55.

Children have also been given the opportunity to discuss, as a class, how they feel about tasks they have completed and to share the emotions of success or, in some cases, failure.* For example, they have reflected on whether or not they felt pressurised at any stage, or found any aspects of a challenge particularly difficult. They have also considered how well they performed as a team, and how individuals contributed to their success in different ways.* As a result of those processes, children have discovered that interpersonal skills and a genuine interest in the ideas and talents of others are at least as important for success as academic ability.

A whole-school approach

* See also the comments by John Kerr ('Silver linings and clouds', page 91); Linda Marshall ('Future plans for Critical Skills ...', page 95) and Bruce Bonney ('Nurturing CSP in Your School', page 122).

It is clear that my own challenge now is to find a way of spreading the principles of CSP beyond the four walls of my own classroom. The challenge appears to be twofold:*

1. How can I best provide training in CSP for all teaching staff at Bruntsfield Primary School?

2. How can we ensure that the principles of CSP become embedded in the curriculum of the school?

Environmental studies developments

I'm currently leading a whole-school development of Environmental Studies, the area of the curriculum that encompasses science, technology and social subjects. While it was anticipated that the development process would be rooted in current good practice, it was also clear that it provided the opportunity to consider ways in which the teaching and learning could be improved and even transformed in the longer term.

There appeared to be several distinct advantages to linking developments in Environmental Studies to staff training in CSP:

→ staff would be given a context in which to consider the ideas and characteristics of CSP

→ staff would be given a framework in which to develop team challenges

→ challenges could be written for children of all ages, covering all aspects of Environmental Studies.

The expectation would be that if staff were given the opportunity to develop the principles of CSP in one area of the curriculum, they would eventually develop the confidence and expertise to apply their newly honed skills to many other areas.

The model of development

I planned a three-year strategy for the development of Environmental Studies, based on a Total Quality Management (TQM) model which shares a number of key features in common with CSP.

The strategy relies on the setting of clear and challenging goals from the outset, and depends on the free flow of information between all members of staff. Teamwork is absolutely central to the process. And in terms of a *collaborative culture*,* it demands the commitment of teachers who have a sense of ownership of the development and share in the vision which drives the process.

* See pages 36–43.

It was clear that staff would need to be equipped with the developmental tools which would allow them to work together successfully to achieve the vision. And that's exactly where CSP came to our aid.*

* Anne Callan describes using the carousel brainstorming tool to help create such a community among her own teaching staff (page 101).

Teachers working together

The first part of an in-service day was devoted to developing teamwork. Forrest Howie and I described our own very positive experiences of CSP training and introduced staff to the four *broad ideas** which underpin the programme as well as the characteristics of a typical CSP classroom.* We also took the opportunity to share examples of collaborative group work which we had developed with our classes.

* See page 33.

* See **Leading the Learning School**, page 73.

Staff organised themselves into teams on the basis of simple *personality indicators** and were introduced to the *Full Value Contract* and the *toolbox*. Equipped with the techniques of *brainstorming and distillation*, and once they had become proficient in the use of the *thumb tool*,* staff were given the challenge of identifying five key features of effective teams, putting those in order of importance, and presenting their ideas to the other groups.

* See the description of group dynamics and the use of the IP3 tool on pages 47–48.

* All of these tools are fully described in 'Creating a collaborative classroom learning community' (pages 36–43).

* See page 53.

Following their presentations, and feedback from the other teams, staff were asked to reflect on the process of reaching their conclusions and to comment on how well they had worked together in their teams. Finally, ideas such as *chunking the challenge** and task roles were introduced.

Developing and sharing the vision

All staff, again working in teams, were given the challenge of identifying what they considered to be the key features of an ideal Environmental Studies programme; to articulate the values which would underpin that programme; and to agree on a vision statement which would guide the process of development. They then presented their ideas at the end of the day and, once again, received feedback from the other teams on the quality of their ideas and the standard of their presentations.

Beyond developing the experience of team challenges further, the eventual aim of this process was to enable staff to articulate a collective vision and set of goals which would drive the subsequent development of the Environmental Studies curriculum.

Planning Environmental Studies

Since then staff have worked together extremely effectively to develop a long-term planning framework for Environmental Studies. As ever in education, timescales have been tight, and the demands on individuals have been significant, but the principles of teamwork, communication and feedback, and the development tools which form the core of CSP, have ensured that progress has been extremely good and that all staff share a sense of ownership of the process.*

* See again Anne Callan's vignette (page 101).

Next year, staff teams will be asked to develop detailed short-term plans for every study identified in the long-term planning framework. We anticipate that at least one team challenge will be built into each study, ensuring that pupils will undertake a minimum of four challenges a year in Environmental Studies from P1 to P7 Further CSP training will be an absolute priority for all teachers at this stage. However, given that they will already have had considerable first-hand experience of the dynamics of teamwork and of CSP methodology I expect them to respond well to this challenge.

Anne Callan – *Headteacher, Murrayfield Primary School, Blackburn, West Lothian*

Introduction

I have been Headteacher at Murrayfield Primary for six years and for the past two years, as part of the development plan, we have been looking at learning and teaching. I am particularly interested in matching teaching styles to learning styles and so became interested in Critical Skills. I have now completed Level 1 and Level 2 training and also have three teachers who have completed Level 1.

After completing Part A of Level 1, myself and a fellow headteacher worked together, looking at how we could use the techniques we had experienced. We decided that CSP would be useful, not only in the classroom, but also as a way of providing in-service training for staff.

Using the model with staff

We were due to look at our school development plan in May 2001 and decided to use the CSP model to complete that. In the interim the McCrone Agreement* came into being, and within our schools we had to gain agreement from our staff to the authority's proposals for implementing it. We also used the CSP model for this.

* This concerned Scottish teachers' conditions of service.

One of the techniques we had used during our own training was *carousel brainstorming*.* We decided that we would use this to help staff define 'autonomous professional teacher' as the professionalism of teaching staff is at the heart of the McCrone Agreement. So we set up three questions:

* See pages 41–43.

1. *What does a professional teacher look like?*
2. *What does a professional teacher sound like?*
3. *What does a professional teacher feel like?*

Staff brainstormed each of these questions. They then had to prioritise their findings; come up with three main points; present their choices to the group; and provide reasons for their choices.

One of the challenges we had been given during training involved each member of our team becoming an 'expert' on an article about education. I felt that many staff had not really read the McCrone Agreement fully, so I took extracts from it, as well as information from the internet and various union publications, to give them information about the agreement.

People within each group then had to become experts on different readings and share their knowledge with each other. From this we reached a greater collective understanding of McCrone and this enabled us to gain agreement to the authority's proposals.* We then identified the time available for curriculum development within the school and moved on with our development plan.

* This was a strikingly successful exercise in both schools, and a vivid demonstration of the power of the CSP model in whole-school, as well as classroom, situations.

Using the model with pupils

At this point I still had not used the CSP model with the children. I felt that what I had tried with the staff had worked very well – but would the same techniques work with the pupils? One Primary 7* class had lost their teacher due to promotion. They now had a supply teacher but were disaffected and unhappy. They began to find fault with each other, with their teachers and with other staff. It became obvious that they needed to do some straight thinking and so I used Critical Skills to work with them. We needed to rebuild their *learning community*.

* Primary 1–7 (P1–7) in Scotland is equivalent to Years 1–7 in England and Wales.

I used the 'Hippo in the Bath' challenge* as a fun way to introduce the carousel brainstorming tool to them. Then we had an open brainstorm to discuss what the problems were within the class. As a result we agreed on four questions:

* 'Hippo in the Bath': A hippo is stuck in a bath. At each of four stations participants have to think of different ways of getting him out, e.g. Station 1 – kind ways; Station 2 – funny ways; Station 3 – expensive ways; Station 4 – politically correct ways!

➡ *What is a quality audience?*
➡ *What is a quality worker?*
➡ *What is a quality teacher?*
➡ *What is a quality friend?*

We then used the carousel brainstorm tool to answer these questions.

* See page 44.

I then gave them the following *challenge** (**Fig. 1**) which required them to work in groups to create a poster, a statement and a set of rules which would be useful to a new member of their team. They had to explain what their values were, and what would be expected of a new team member.

Transforming Teaching & Learning

Figure 1. Values challenge

Values Challenge

Challenge: A new person coming into your class team has to know what you, as a class, value. Use the carousel tool to brainstorm the following issues:

➡ *What is a quality friend?*
➡ *What is a quality audience?*
➡ *What is a quality worker?*
➡ *What is a quality teacher?*

Within your group look at the suggestions made during the 'quality' carousel.

➡ Produce a poster which depicts your group's 'quality'.
➡ Produce a statement which describes your group's 'quality'.
➡ Produce a set of rules which would help someone to fit your group's 'quality'.
➡ Present your findings, as a group, to the rest of the class.

Product criteria:

➡ Your poster must contain an illustration, describe your 'quality' and tell a new team member what you value.
➡ Your statement must describe your 'quality', make use of the brainstorming ideas and be easily read.
➡ Your rules must be easily read and understood by everyone and be positive (no negatives; tell what people have to do, not what they have not to do).

Presentation criteria:

➡ You must display your products.
➡ Everyone in the group must speak.
➡ Everyone in the group has to be introduced.
➡ You must explain the task.
➡ You must say what conclusions you reached.
➡ You must 'talk to' your products.

Resources:

➡ felt markers
➡ carousel sheets
➡ A1 paper
➡ A3 paper
➡ Blu-tack

Timescale: You have only 45 minutes until presentation time.* The presentation should last no longer than 7 minutes.

Good luck!

* Note the emphasis on a time limit. This is a characteristic feature of CSP and relates to development of the critical skill of organisation, one of the key indicators of which is 'optimising time and resources'.

* See 'What the teacher does: C – Feedback and Assessment', (pages 60–62).

* See 'Peer assessment' (page 57).

* See 'Using the IP3 tool' (pages 47–48).

* **How Good is Our School? Self-Evaluation Using Performance Indicators** was published in 1996 by the then Scottish Office Education and Industry Department Audit Unit.

* See page 40.

* Several other headteachers have reported this effect. And Gilboa-Conesville Central School has been totally transformed by use of the model at all levels of the school, as described in some detail in Chapter 5 of **Leading the Learning School**. Network Educational Press now organises CSP institutes for Senior Management, run by Bruce Bonney and Matt Murray, Superintendent of Gilboa-Conesville.

I used an *observation checklist** to monitor the pupils' work. The pupils themselves used a *huddle* to get together after each group's presentation and give constructive feedback.* We also used an IP3 to debrief the challenge.* The whole activity was a great success. I went home that night 'walking on air'!

At this point my colleague headteacher and I were asked to give a presentation about CSP to a West Lothian Council working party which was looking at continuing professional development in the light of the McCrone Agreement. We described the CSP model, our current level of expertise, and gave examples of our practice before proposing a way forward for our schools and West Lothian in general.

As a result of this presentation I now have three members of staff who have trained to Level 1 and are using the model in class. We have found that it sits very well with Personal and Social Development work and can be used in any area of the curriculum.

I myself have now completed Level 2 training and am currently writing a 'rubric' which will be used to monitor teaching and learning across the school. A rubric is the CSP term for a scoring tool that lists the criteria for a piece of work. I am linking the rubric to the performance indicators in *How Good is our School?**

When holding assemblies I can now ask for a *quality audience** and get it immediately. I am slowly introducing terms and tools at assemblies to promote interest among pupils and staff. I have also had calls from colleagues in other schools expressing interest in the programme.

I believe that Critical Skills will prove to be invaluable in school and that it can be applied to learning at any stage. In my own establishment we eventually hope to use it from Nursery to P7 and also for in-service training. I have also found the tools and techniques invaluable in the management of the school.*

'And the best thing – it works!'

Rick Lee – *Raising Achievement Co-ordinator, Barrow-in-Furness Community Learning Partnership*

Introduction

Halfway through Part B of my Level 1 CSP training course I was driving home late. A blood-red moon was rising over Morecambe Bay and three badgers were suddenly gambolling along the road in front of me. A Celtic shaman would no doubt have been able to tell me the meaning of this strange and exhilarating experience. However, I don't need such ancient or arcane wisdom to spot the significance and potential of my experience of Critical Skills training!

As a Raising Achievement Co-ordinator I was responsible for organising this training for Barrow Community Learning Partnership – a second round Education Action Zone – in conjunction with Network Educational Press. The effect on the 22 teachers involved was one of the most influential and dramatic responses we have seen during our efforts to provide opportunities to access new teaching and learning strategies. The most immediate evidence of this is the rapid take-up from these teachers' schools for places in the second round of training.

This eagerness to grab places – requiring two or three teachers to be out of each school for six days each in total – is set within the context of a desperate teacher and supply shortage in the Barrow area. During the second part of the first Level 1 training institute, teachers came despite the imminence of SATs, and one teacher even turned down an interview opportunity! At the end of the course we were mentally exhausted, yet happy – a strong community of revitalised practitioners determined not to let these critical skills slip through our fingers and deprive us of using them to their full potential.

The training experience

'So what,' one imagines the staffroom cynic might say, 'have you lot been doing skiving off in the sunshine while the rest of us have been grinding away at the chalkface?' One of my course colleagues was indeed asked this in the pub and had the foresight to say that he was quite happy to share his experiences, but not in the pub, not in five minutes, and not in response to such an obviously cynical tone of voice!

So what is the Critical Skills Programme and why has it had such a profound effect on a whole group of teachers? I should also point out that this was a very 'mixed ability' group. We had NQTs, a headteacher, experienced and inexperienced, reception through to KS4, different subject specialists and a wide range of pedagogical understanding and beliefs. We worked individually, in pairs, small groups and as a whole group of 22 – constantly regrouping and forming different relationships.

CSP tools and techniques

* Linda Marshall (page 92) and Brian Speedie (page 97) also make the same point.

Much of what we used we felt we already knew or would regard as part of our teacher toolkit. The most influential and revealing factor was the way in which lots of good practice had been synthesised into a holistic approach, which we could see had immense power.*

* See the margin note at the end of Anne Callan's vignette (page 104).

Many of us, for example, are experienced problem-solving facilitators and have used Socratic questioning techniques and more formalised strategies such as 'Mantle of the Expert' for many years. But here was a whole-class – potentially whole-school* – approach which could transform classrooms and attitudes to life-long learning in a dramatic and sustainable way.

* See pages 38–40. See also Anne Callan's comments about the effectiveness of the **quality audience** tool (page 104).

Probably the two most effective – yet simple and obvious – tools which we adopted were our written and displayed agreements (that is, contracts) about what for us constituted a *quality discussion* and a *quality audience*.* For us the important aspects of these two crucial, community-building tools were:

➡ we discussed them in small groups and then synthesised them

➡ we wrote them down

➡ we put them on the wall

➡ we referred to them constantly.

And by and large we stuck to them – and what a difference it made to the quality of our discussions and the respect we gave each other in debate and towards our presentations. I think the quality of debate in staffrooms and staff meetings would be improved immeasurably by the introduction of these agreements and I try to encourage this. Teachers on the course have told me about the dramatic and sustainable improvements that these helped to bring about in the social health of their classes.*

*See, for example, Heather Swinson's observation (page 86) that the HM Inspector 'noted that this programme could be considered as part of an early intervention scheme'.

Challenges galore

Once this atmosphere had been set from the start we then engaged in a series of more and more demanding *challenges** – each one tackling a different technique or introducing us to the various *critical skills* and *fundamental dispositions*.

* See page 44 and page 32.

We spent time looking at the four different *decision-making styles*.* We laughed at and enjoyed the revelations about our personal decision-making preferences and dislikes – but we also learned to use them efficiently when working on a challenge. This became particularly critical as we began to realise the seemingly ridiculously short times allocated to the completion of tasks! Soon we began to work at a terrific speed, learning to *chunk the challenge* and allocate time and resources efficiently* – particularly using people's talents and preferred working styles, while also recognising their reluctances and supporting their apprehensions.

* See 'Using the IP3 tool', pages 47–48.

* See page 53.

We became aware of the vital yet at times frustrating and time-consuming necessity to grope and gripe our way through the storming and denial stages of group dynamics. As a drama specialist of 25 years' experience I think I have considerable awareness of group dynamics, and a whole array of techniques honed in the forge of improvisation and classroom conflict. Yet I'd not brought it all together in the way that this programme does.*

* Yet another comment about the way in which CSP provides such a comprehensive and powerful framework for bringing together a wide range of effective ideas and techniques.

Our *scenario challenge* on the fifth day was to make a presentation to an invited audience of educationists and business people. We were given the challenge on the previous afternoon, about 15 minutes before the end of a very hard day during which there had been a particularly difficult hour of griping and storming. We were all emotionally and intellectually drained, and quite a few confessed that they'd gone home less than certain that we would be able to complete this challenge successfully.*

* This is a very common phenomenon but, as Bruce Bonney says, 'Real learning is always at the edge of our comfort zone'! (page 129).

The next morning we only had two-and-a-half hours. If you conjure up the images of burning brains and fingers you would not be far away from picturing the level of industry and intense collaborative endeavour achieved in that short time. Suffice to say that the main criticism of our presentation from the panel was that we gave them too much information and bewildered them with the breadth of our knowledge. They also said that there was no mistaking our commitment and belief in this methodology, and that within the frame of the scenario they had no hesitation in awarding us the extra funds.

Assessment

On the final day we were challenged to debate assessment. We were very tired by now,* but again the challenge was revealing. We were asked to synthesise four lengthy articles about assessment issues, and present them to each other. This was conducted at a high level of pedagogical debate and it was only afterwards that I reflected that all the articles were from the US and that I'm not aware of this level of debate in the UK. We

* Note that in CSP classrooms it is typical for pupils to end the day feeling more tired than their teachers. Isn't this how it should be? But how often is it precisely the opposite?!

* Many of the US articles used for the early rounds of UK training have now been replaced by UK equivalents. In the case of assessment, much emphasis is given to Black and Wiliam' **Inside the Black Box: Raising Standards Through Classroom Assessment** (King's College London, 1998).

* This issue is discussed in some depth in **Leading the Learning School** (pages 40–44: 'Misleading Mental Models').

seem as a profession to have largely given up the fight against grading, setting and rankings – despite the fact that most of the research evidence indicates that these approaches are at best unhelpful and at worst counterproductive.*

Critical Skills leads us to an assessment approach that doesn't evade or ignore the thorny issues of subjectivity or teacher competence. It requires teachers to work together with pupils, to facilitate useful self-assessment; to encourage supportive peer group assessment; to make the assessment criteria transparent, credible and understandable; and above all to make the whole process authentic for both teacher and pupil.

It also asks some very demanding questions about setting and grouping pupils horizontally by age or ability. These questions add weight to the increasing awareness that we have about the way the brain functions, multiple intelligences and preferred ways of working. This should make us work hard to break out of the straitjacket of attitudes which are often just plain wrong.*

Conclusion: a journey of educational endeavour

We must, however, remember that the process of change requires us to go through that process of 'groping, griping, storming and denial' which all heroes of change must undergo; and that some of us are more inclined to tread the path with vigour and enthusiasm than others. I may read the red moon as the triumph of a revolution in educational thinking and practice; and the three gambolling badgers as the freeing of youthful and natural energy. Others might simply see trouble and doom, brought about by TB-carrying vermin.

My title is a deliberate reference to an article written by Dorothy Heathcote in 1978. Dorothy has had an immense impact on the teaching and learning of some drama specialists and other teachers, but her own thinking has been largely ignored by educationists in this country – a costly and unfortunate example of a prophet being unheard in her own land. Her article provided us with a pedagogical and practical blueprint for using drama as a learning medium – both as a way of teaching the drama form and as a way of intriguing pupils into curriculum materials and issues.

These strategies have much in common with the scenario challenges and classroom ethos created using the CSP model. It has disappointed me that these strategies are unknown to many teachers who could use them effectively in their day-to-day teaching, whatever phase or subject they teach. I hope that such a fate does not befall Critical Skills and that this article and the commitment of Network Educational Press will act as a clear signpost to others on the journey of educational endeavour.

Jo Morrison – *Lecturer, Tresham Institute of Further and Higher Education, Kettering, Northants*

Introduction

It's 3.15pm on a bleak October afternoon. I'm exhausted after two hours with the 'box of frogs' – so called because I'd just get one settled when another would jump out. I've lost count of the times I've said 'Please don't swear at ... please sit down ... please don't stab Jackie* with that knife ... (give it to me and *I'll* do it) ...' What remains of my class has left the computer suite, their terminals still live, mobiles in hand. As they walk down the corridor outside they're thumping the walls of the suite, shrieking at each other.

* Unsurprisingly, the names of all the students in this article have been changed!

A colleague who's working with a group of adults at the other end of the room quietly, and with sympathy, tells me of the complaints from her class about my class's noise, language and attitude. 'Honestly, Jo, if you can't control them you'll have to find somewhere else to take them in the future.' Last straw. At least I'd kept *some* of them in the room – which was a first.

I went home and cried all over Rob. You know the scenario: 'What am I doing? Is it worth it? Am I making a difference?...' This was the sixth time in six Tuesdays. 'Nobody should have to put up with this, love. Just refuse to teach them.'

The last time a colleague had complained about my discipline (lack of, that is) had been in my second year of teaching. That was 25 years ago! I was mortified *then*, and the resonance was hugely discomfiting. But for me to refuse to teach a group of students was unthinkable.

It was then that I realised that 'The Frogs' were the most challenging kids I'd ever faced – and I've taught in what used to be called 'approved schools', in schools for the then termed 'maladjusted', and more recently on the 'New Start' initiatives for disaffected and excluded students. I'm the woman who says that they're not problem kids, they're kids with problems. I'm the woman who loves to work with the disinterested and disaffected. I'm the woman who claims to be able to teach anything to anyone. The Frogs didn't seem to appreciate that, though. In fact, The Frogs thought I was 'pants', and told me so – regularly. I'd lost my sense of humour. Time to stop teaching.

We need some history at this point. In September 2000 Further Education gained a new and surprising intake. We've traditionally had extensive provision for Special Needs

post-16 students, and then for GCSE retakes – but nothing in between. Suddenly, we had a whole load of students who didn't have specific learning difficulties, but who hadn't made it to the GCSE plateau. In my college, my friend and colleague Pam invented and wrote a course called 'Fresh Start' to fill the gap. Essentially, this involved enrolling the students on vocational courses while giving them loads of Key Skills support as infrastructure.

We started to interview. We saw a whole range of applicants: school refusers; ex-New Start people; people in long-term residential therapeutic care; people seeking asylum. You name it. They all had one thing in common – they hadn't achieved in the traditional sense. 'Marvellous' I thought, 'right up my alley.' My role was Key Skills support.

One incident on Enrolment Day sums up our intake. We were filling in the registration forms when this lad Darren walked in. He was about six foot three, with a shaven head with tattoos at the front. He'd got so much ironmongery in his face and tongue that I tried, unsuccessfully, not to exercise my imagination about the rest of his piercings...

He had a thong wound round his right arm, which was also liberally decorated with tattoos. He was wearing an Iron Maiden T-shirt and combat trousers, whose pockets were bulging with other people's possessions. Laboriously we filled in his name and address on the registration form. The next question was 'Last school attended'. He hailed from The Arbours, a beautiful name disguising a school for behaviourally challenging pupils.

'I'm not fillin' that bit in, Jo,' he said.

'That's OK,' I replied, 'and why's that?'

'Well. It might give the wrong impression...'

Then there was Pierre, whose sister came with him to translate. He was a small boy whose speech I still find hard to comprehend.

'You have arrived from Monserrat? Why on earth do you want to come to Kettering from Monserrat?' Geography was never Pam's strong point.

'It got a bit hot there...' his sister stated, drily. Ah. Comprehension dawned – too late. Volcanic activity. Widespread misery... Not a good start.

Transforming Teaching & Learning

And so it went on. Every single applicant had a past. There was Jackie, who was so difficult to handle that her mum handed her over to Social Services – when she was six! There was John, in long-term residential care at 17, very bright but very aggressive.

There was Laura, dark, pretty and terminally lazy; she was a school refuser who missed the day they did maths, who wouldn't come to college unless her mum drove her there and picked her up at the drop of a mobile call. There was Sebastian from the Gambia, who was aloof from the silly antics of the rest but who wouldn't communicate.

Then there were Sam'n'Eric, two girls I named after the *Lord of the Flies* characters, in danger of being ignored because they were (initially) quiet and nice and at the mercy of the rest of the group. Then there was A. N. Other, who was so easy that he got no attention whatsoever.

Which brings us back to the bleak October afternoon. Darren and John had walked out at 1.35pm on the grounds that they were there to learn effin' Leisure and Tourism, not effin' IT and English. Laura had resorted to her well-honed avoidance strategy; she felt unwell and phoned her mum to fetch her. Jackie sat playing on the chat lines until I suggested that perhaps she might engage with the work I'd set. Clearly this was unreasonable on my part so she left – after creating ten minutes of mayhem. Pierre, Sam'n'Eric, Sebastian and ANO lethargically played the education game* until I released them.

I'd read a *really* good book during the summer. One sentence made a huge impact. It read: 'What do they know when they leave the room that they didn't know before they came in?' I remember disconsolately walking round, turning off the machines, thinking that all they'd learned during that session were more strategies to wind me up. For example, Darren discovered, before he left, that Christians like me would go completely reptilian when confronted with horrid stuff like satanic websites and conversations about a film whose title I can't bring myself to write!

Anyway, this was the week before half term so I cheered myself up with the thought that I was off to New York State on Saturday. This trip was prompted by a one-day conference I'd attended during the summer about the State's Critical Skills Programme initiative. Fascinated by this, yet unusually cynical, I decided to go and check out the schools* featured on the video shown during the course, and also do the preliminary three days' CSP training.

I won't bore you with the details of the training – others have already written about that* – but it was brilliant! The school visits provided compelling evidence that the scheme worked. The kids were friendly, polite(!) and collaborative; and their standard of work refreshingly high. So I spent the Thursday afternoon session planning (in America) for my Monday classes (in Kettering). It was hard work, I can tell you, but infinitely more fun than usual, sitting on the floor surrounded by flipchart paper and loads of pens.

So I came back at the end of the October half term, and started to teach the new way. I told the students I was unhappy; that the current situation wasn't working, and that I was going to try something different.

* 'The game is called "Let's Pretend", and if its name were chiselled into the front of every school building ... we would at least have an honest announcement of what takes place there. The game is based on a series of pretences which include: let's pretend that ... this sort of work makes a difference to your lives; let's pretend that what bores you is important, and that the more you are bored, the more important it is...' (**Teaching as a Subversive Activity** by N. Postman and C. Weingartner, Penguin, 1969)

* The main school featured in the video was Gilboa-Conesville Central – see Pete Fox's vignette (page 66).

* See, for example, Section 3, vignettes 4, 5 and 9.

* This exactly parallels Pete Fox's experience (page 69), as well as that of many other CSP trainees.

* See pages 60–62.

Within two weeks, colleagues were asking me what was happening.* How come the students were so different? (These were colleagues who'd previously described these kids as 'unteachable'.) This wasn't down to me. Honestly, the kids drove it.

The key thing for me was the structure which underpins the CSP model. Others have described the underpinning tools of the model, but two things in particular created change in my classroom. The first was the overt emphasis laid on the *skills* I want my students to exhibit – as opposed to *knowledge* alone. The second was the range of feedback mechanisms, which held up a mirror to my students.*

This mirror has been unforgiving, and illuminating for the students, in a manner which I haven't experienced for at least 15 years. The debriefing sessions which follow the completion of each challenge provide a vehicle through which the students examine their own behaviour and contribution to their groups.

So the particular skill areas I targeted at the outset were 'working collaboratively' and 'working as a member of a group'. These kids were not a group, merely a collection of individuals hell-bent on putting each other – and me – down. In order to be successful at work and at life in general, they had to learn to get along with other people. **Figure 1** (below) shows one feedback tool that we used to encourage the students to reflect on their progress in developing these skills.

Figure 1. Review and reflection: A self-assessment sheet

Helping each other to achieve a common goal
Mark Scheme

My Name: _____   My Class: _____   My Total Score: _____

Me and my team

I helped my team to decide what we were aiming to achieve.	1	2	3	4	5
I was committed to reaching this goal.	1	2	3	4	5
I helped to 'chunk the challenge'.	1	2	3	4	5
I helped decide who was going to do what.	1	2	3	4	5
I helped decide when each person had to finish his/her task.	1	2	3	4	5
I helped and encouraged each member of my team.	2	4	6	8	10

Me on my own

I made sure I understood what I had to do.	1	2	3	4	5
I completed my own task on time.	1	2	3	4	5
I did it as well as I possibly could.	1	2	3	4	5
I asked my team to help me if I got stuck.	1	2	3	4	5
I helped other people if they asked me.	1	2	3	4	5

Me and the challenge

We completed the challenge on time.	2	4	6	8	10
We worked together as a team.	2	4	6	8	10
We sorted out our conflicts without asking Jo too much.	2	4	6	8	10

Max score = 90   Ring what you think YOU scored in blue or black.   I'll ring what I think you scored in red.

Figures 2–4 show examples of early challenges I used with them to achieve the objectives set out in Figure 1. A surprising side effect was that, although I obtained loads of English, maths and IT accreditation from these and other challenges, the students didn't notice that they were achieving 'Key Skills' – so that ended the conflict between my (irrelevant) subjects and their chosen vocational options. They responded to Real Life Challenges immediately and with relish. It was fantastic!

Figure 2 was the first challenge of the year, and introduces the tools of *quality listening* and *quality discussion*. It is based on one of the challenges in the CSP training.*

* See the 'team challenge' on page 52.

Figure 2

Knowledge Accreditation for: Wordpower IT Working with others	**Academic Challenge** A Fresh Start	Skills The skills of: Communication Research Self Assessment

Induction Challenge
Completion Date:

Problem:	Who are we? What strengths can we bring to the course to make it a successful experience for all of us?
Challenge:	In your group, you are going to create a team which may work together in the future. You are going to introduce your team, by name, to the other teams. Please prepare a presentation (5 mins. max) for the rest of us. You will: ● provide us with information about what people want from the college/why you are here ● identify two behaviours your team thinks will be important for us to exhibit if we are to be successful on the course ● tell us what strengths your team will be able to contribute to the group ● provide information about your goals ● create a graphic or logo which sums your team up.
Product marking guide	*Rule*: Presentations read by – *Form*: All members involved. Presentation to the point, clear and entertaining. *Content*: 5 mins max. Names given. Strengths identified. Behaviours identified. Biographical details given. Logo created.
Evidence of: knowledge/skill	● A base of interpersonal info is built up which will support our collaborative work. We will look/listen for teams referring to each other by name, relating to each other in terms of common experience. ● Speaking and listening supportively, checking understanding. We will look/listen for a quality conversation and quality listeners.

Figure 3 was our second challenge, and the one which Jackie led. They had about three weeks to plan it, raise the money, and organize the journey. It worked like a charm. Not only did it create tons of Key Skills assessment – we also had a day's shopping in Milton Keynes. In addition, they bought toys for ITV's 'This Morning' Christmas appeal.

Figure 3

Knowledge Accreditation for: Wordpower Numberpower IT Working with others	**Real Life Challenge** Fresh Start - Further Steps	**Skills** The skills of: Confirming my own responsibilities Working with others to achieve the challenge Identify progress, and how to improve my work

Problem:	Working, as a group, to achieve a common goal: to go on a day out.
Challenge	Pam and Jo want to take you somewhere really nice for one day. We will take you there if you complete the challenge. Here it is: In your WHOLE group, decide where you'd like to go... OK. After that you need to do these things: ● research, cost and book the place ● work out transportation, and costs – the Institute has rules about the minibus ● find out the Institute's rules about outside visits ● raise the money to pay for it.
Product marking guide	**Rule**: Due in by – **Form**: a diary of your activities day by day ● summary of rules for outside visits ● permission letter to parents with a tear-off reply slip ● to-scale route map with mileage ● list of expenses ● summary of your fundraising ideas.
Evidence of: knowledge/skill	Letter-writing, diary-writing, scale drawing, profit and loss accounts, working with others, meeting your own responsibilities, initiative.

The challenge shown in **Figure 4** was a cracking idea. Jackie and chums had horrible views about disabled people. The IT group which taught them Powerpoint included, among others, a couple of autistic students, one with cerebral palsy, a wheelchair user, and a person with visual impairment. Their ideas that disabled people were also stupid were overturned by this challenge. It also enabled the IT group to teach another group. One of the most powerful ways of learning is to teach somebody else.

Figure 4

Knowledge Accreditation for: Written communication Measuring time Summarising information	**Academic Challenge** A Fresh Start	**Skills** The skills of: Listening Working with others Interpersonal skills Valuing others

Leisure and Tourism
Completion Date:

Problem:	Pam and Jo want to use a Powerpoint presentation to explain Fresh Start–Further Steps.

Challenge	You are going to be taught by the Fresh Start IT group to use Powerpoint. You will have to: ● work with the IT students to learn Powerpoint ● listen and watch what they show you ● ask appropriate questions if you do not understand ● act in an appropriate way ● make them feel welcome ● assess how well they have helped you.

Product marking guide	You will have to: ● produce slides explaining the course ● include appropriate pictures and text ● write a script that will accompany the slides ● time the presentation to last for at least 15 minutes ● give the presentation to a member of staff ● be assessed by the IT students on your level of skill.

Evidence of: **knowledge/skill**	Wordpower, numberpower, working with others, equal opportunities. Working TOGETHER with other people towards a common goal. Communication with other people. Interpersonal skills, friendliness, politeness, consideration.

Several incidents will live with me forever, and can still raise the hairs on the back of my neck. At the end of the first challenge (which they failed) we brainstormed the reasons for their failure. Without intervention from me, the students came up with things like: *'We need to listen'*, *'We need to plan'*, *'We need to take on individual responsibility'*.

Then Darren said it was Jackie's fault because she was 'assing about'. I wish I had a photograph of her face at that moment (*specific observable behaviour!*). I'd told her the same thing, in more 'teachery' terms, for over a year. But coming from a member of her peer group it suddenly had real impact.

So I made her the leader of her group for the next challenge. I told her that she'd got an hour to succeed. She was determined. She got cross when they were all talking at once and demanded a mechanism whereby they could signal if they wanted to speak. John suggested they raise their hands. 'Brilliant idea' she said!! Then Laura turned to the chat lines and Jackie was FURIOUS and told her to stop being rude. I raised my eyebrows from the sidelines. The gesture was not lost; taking an uncharacteristically long time to pack her bag at the end of the session, Jackie came up to me when they'd all gone. 'That was what being a teacher's like,' she said.

'Yep.'

'Ah ... sorry,' she muttered. You could have knocked me down with the proverbial. I turned away to hide my tears. She misinterpreted this.

'No, I am,' she insisted. 'You've always been dead nice to me and I've been right in your face.'

By the end of June they were a different bunch of kids. They were working together, trying really hard not to make staff unhappy – and running up to my car as I parked to say 'hello' and to open the door for me.

The fact that we had retained them at all speaks volumes in the FE sector. It has been a steep learning curve, and incredibly hard work, but so worth it that Pam and I haven't minded the hours of planning. It's in place now, and we can fine-tune it as the years progress. We won the college prize for retention of students. OfSTED was impressed by CSP, especially its emphasis on individual target-setting and debriefing mechanisms.

Figure 5 shows a student writing a journal entry – now typical of our students. I wouldn't have dared even to ask them to do this when we started?

Figure 5

> 24.9.02
>
> During my Induction Challenge I think I worked well at communicating with the members of my group and also giving eye contact. I think that I could improve on speaking slower by taking my time. As a group I think we all done well at communicating and meeting the deadline because we done it on time by exactly 3 minutes, but I do think that we could improve on the presentation by practising more. We ensured that all the group ideas were heard by taking turns to speak we also made sure that they were involved by asking them if they had my ideas. We made sure that the Challenge went smoothly by setting targets so everybody knew what they were doing. We ensured that it was a quality product by producing a checklist.

I personally believe that CSP is THE way forward for education in the UK.* It speaks to kids in a way that I personally haven't found before, through all the initiatives with which I've been involved. It is broken, and we need to mend it. This is the repair kit.

* So do many other CSP practitioners. See, for example, the quote from Di Buck of SUCCESS@EAZ, Bristol, on page 174.

Bruce Bonney

1. Staying Alive with CSP: Advice for Newly Trained CSP Teachers

2. CSP in Your School: Greenhouse or Gobi? Advice for Senior Managers

3. Frequently Asked Questions

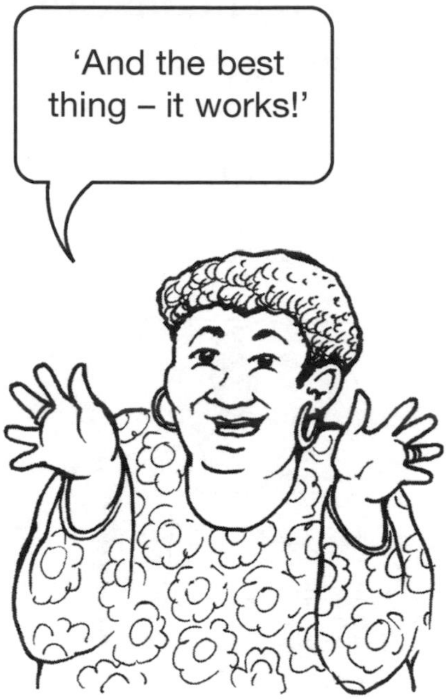
'And the best thing – it works!'

1. Staying Alive with CSP: Advice for Newly Trained Critical Skills Teachers

Introduction

At one time I believed it wouldn't be too difficult. It was a matter of awareness, of getting the word out, of letting my colleagues know there really was an alternative to the traditional structure of teaching and learning that we'd all grown to know and accept throughout our lives in school. When I saw my students 'get it' in my classroom, I assumed that any observer would recognize the power inherent in the CSP classroom approach – the quality of experience, the depth of the learning.

Granted, not every single student responded positively to CSP. But overwhelmingly more students learned at a deeper level and with greater skill than with any approach I had used previously. I thought any educator worthy of the name who understood CSP would certainly leap at the chance to empower their students with these skills, enrich their lives with these challenges. All they needed was to see it; to get some decent modelling and guidance; perhaps a smattering of support and encouragement. A movement would grow, change would occur – one teacher, one classroom, one school, one state at a time. Surely, if we built it, they would come.

That was a decade ago. And obviously, the acceptance and growth of CSP in my school, my region, and certainly within the state of New York has not evolved in quite the tidy, linear fashion I envisioned.

The following are some distilled insights of an educator who first used the CSP model in his own classroom (13–18-year-old students); then left school to work for the Critical Skills/Education by Design Program, teaching teachers throughout New England; and most recently has used the model to build an organisation/business to spread CSP in New York State.

Perhaps more importantly, however, these are the musings of a Newtonian mind struggling to grasp (forget control) the chaos of what I grudgingly now accept to be the quantum universe of educational change.

'Walking the talk'

Before I offer any sage advice on how to make CSP work for you, I think I should make clear my underlying perspective on this model.

As I understand it, the CSP model is a coherent and effective framework for high-quality, collaborative problem-solving, period!

It isn't just about transforming teaching and learning in classrooms. I see it as much more. I see its principles and practices as applicable to any gathering of folks (family, teaching staff, community organisation, education authority, business organisation, and so on) who want to work together to produce high-quality solutions to complex challenges – like raising our children, reforming our church, reinventing our school, creating a successful business, allocating our governmental resources, and so on.

* The great J. Edwards Deming, father of the Japanese post-war 'economic miracle', maintained that 'principles are indivisible'. And this is the underlying theme of **Leading the Learning School** which describes how the CSP model can be used to transform schools at all levels, in the way that happened at Gilboa-Conesville Central School (see Pete Fox's vignette, page 66).

Perhaps this vision sounds a tad grandiose. OK, participants in some of our institutes have teased us over the years for having a touch of the missionary about us. Yet I know from scores of observations and hundreds of conversations with people I trust, that this model works – in and out of the classroom – to transform groups of diverse people into highly effective, collaborative problem-solving teams.*

This perspective places a special burden on me as a practitioner and overt proponent of this model. More than anything else, my association with CSP over the years has prompted me to reflect on the way my own knowledge, skill and dispositions have an impact on others around me. If we ask others to reflect on their own performance often enough, inevitably we must turn the mirror on ourselves.

How well do I listen to the ideas of others? Do I let others know I value their contributions? Am I doing the best job I can, given the resources available? These questions and others become part of the experience of everyone I know who has stayed with this model for long.

Our challenge, then, as practitioners committed to this approach, is to find ways to model the model at every opportunity – both in our personal lives and within the structure of the organisations we hope to lead.

Now, to some specifics.

Nurturing CSP in your school

If you are a novice CSP practitioner seeking to use this model in your school, here are some thoughts you might consider.

You already know that implementing CSP in your own classroom stretches many of your professional capacities. Developing a supportive environment for CSP to grow in your school may be even more challenging.

* Note that, although Pete Fox was the only CSP trainee in Gilboa to start with, he was supported by his senior managers. 'Our superintendent and principal gave us full support... Most important, they themselves took the programme and began to conduct our staff meetings in a CSP format' (page 69).

In my experience, a single CSP practitioner in a school without a sustaining network of sympathetic colleagues is a formula for martyrdom.* It is very important that you find ways to create the kind of environment in your school that will give you the opportunity to go through the normal cycle of learning experiences that any novice requires. *Please remember that all the principles we know about optimal learning conditions for our students apply to us as well!* – that is as physically and emotionally safe environment, opportunities to see models and guided practice, supportive and informative feedback, time for reflection, and so on.

How can we start to create these conditions for ourselves in our school?

1. Start quietly and small

Most participants emerge from a Level 1 institute just as we hope – filled with enthusiasm and eager to try out and share their new ideas and strategies.* Unfortunately, this very enthusiasm can backfire on them when they return to school. Depending on the organisational culture, new ideas may be welcomed and supported; ignored; or discouraged and even attacked as threatening. Sometimes all three responses occur within the same institution!

In general, I suggest that you maintain a relatively low profile as you try out the CSP approach in your own learning environment (classroom, school staff, and so on), proceeding at your own level of comfort. Give yourself and your learners some time to understand and develop skill with the model.

Keep interested parties informed of your work but try to refrain from raising expectations too fast or too soon. Please note that this advice is a great example of 'Do as I say, not as I did'! Some of us have a personality that is not noted for doing things quietly or small. In that case 'Go for it' – and be of good cheer!

A corollary to this advice is the necessity to be candid in your appraisal of events. Sometimes things work brilliantly, and other times they are a mess. When asked, let others know the range of your experience. CSP is by no means a perfect or the 'one and only' approach to effective teaching and learning. **Part of the high credibility of our programme is our willingness to acknowledge imperfection, reflect on it, and move on to try and do better next time. Modelling this attitude and pattern of behaviour is central to encouraging it in others.***

2. Seek out friends and allies

As noted above, debriefing and reflecting on our CSP experience is crucial to our growth as a learner. We encourage schools and authorities to send teams of educators to our institutes so that our graduates have a trusted colleague whom they can talk to upon returning to school.*

Lacking this, you will want to find someone sympathetic and willing to listen to your thoughts about your experience. Your 'ear' need not be trained in CSP nor even an educator, although understanding the realities of classroom life helps tremendously. They will, however, need to be skilled in the art of listening, and willing to let you work out the full range of emotions you are experiencing as a novice with the model.

Beyond developing a personal network within your learning environment, you will no doubt want advice from more experienced CSP people at some point. Use telecommunications (phone, email, internet) to contact and collaborate with other CSP educators in your immediate area or farther away. CSP is now present on two continents. No doubt you can find some CSP proponent out there who will be more than willing to assist.*

* For example: 'As a young teacher I felt enthused, empowered and revitalised' (Forrest Howie – page 75). 'By the end of the week I was hooked! I returned to school, hoping for an opportunity to put into practice some of what I had learned' (Heather Swinson – page 83).

* See also John Kerr's comments on page 31.

* Rick Lee's vignette describes how the experience of a group of 22 teachers from the same authority was particularly powerful and beneficial, viz: 'At the end of the course we were mentally exhausted, yet happy – a strong community of revitalised practitioners determined not to let these critical skills slip through our fingers...' (page 105).

* The CSP website (www.criticalskills.co.uk) enables all CSP trainees to maintain full contact and exchange information. Note, too, the advantage of being part of a Level 1 'package' group in terms of networking with colleagues. (See Rick Lee's comments above.)

3. Use results to build a constituency for your approach

Decision-makers who bear the cost of sending their staff to CSP institutes want and need some results to justify their investment. This is not an unreasonable expectation so long as all involved have a mutual understanding of what constitutes results in a CSP classroom, and an appreciation of the time frame involved.

Many senior managers have little experience or understanding of CSP. It is highly likely that they have no grasp of the desired outcomes of the programme or what expectations are appropriate to have of a teacher who is a novice in using the methodology. It is therefore highly desirable for CSP graduates to have an extended conversation with their managers to educate them about the implications of this model for their classroom practice.*

* This is one of the issues addressed in the newly designed CSP Senior Management Institutes (see the margin note at the end of Anne Callan's vignette – page 104).

I strongly suggest that somewhere in the conversation with your manager you say to her/him: 'When you come to my classroom, please look and/or listen for the following evidence of my novice level of implementation of the CSP methodology.' You should then have a thorough discussion of the relevant performance indicators, so that both of you are comfortable with the arrangement.

Following an observation period, you will want to debrief the experience in terms of the same set of indicators. Without such a conversation, your manager will probably use a totally inappropriate set of criteria to guide her/his observation of your work, with predictable results.

The need to demonstrate results rarely stops with school managers, however. Colleagues, parents, other school staff, and local authority officials all may want to know what is going on in your room, and call on you to justify your pedagogy.

Here is where many of the CSP tools and techniques for gathering data about student performance can be of help. Keep anecdotal records* of student behaviour so that you can describe, document, and track the growth you see as your students develop their skills. Retain a selection of students' 'End-of-the-Day' log sheets (see **Fig. 1**) or written debriefing responses as evidence of student thinking. Display student products in public places, along with the criteria for quality, so that observers see that quality work is at the heart of everything you do.

* See page 60.

Send notes or letters home to parents informing them of your students' work.* Be sure to explain that you are placing equal emphasis on student mastery of both content and life-long *critical skills*. If traditional testing is a major concern in your environment, keep records of student scores so that you have a baseline for comparison over time.*

* See the passage on 'Spreading the word' in Forrest Howie's vignette (page 75).

* See, for example, Fig. 1 in Pete Fox's vignette (page 70).

In short, anticipate that at some point in your development as a CSP practitioner you will eventually have to support your professional judgement about this model with some reasonably credible documented evidence. No doubt this will stretch your administrative skills. However, collecting evidence a little at a time on your terms is infinitely preferable to a frantic search for data later on when pressed to justify yourself on less friendly terms.

Figure 1 (See also pages 55 and 117.)

Learning Log

Name: _____ Class: _____ Date: _____

Please write your thoughts on at least 3 of the following questions

What I learned was...
What I found interesting about this work was...
What surprised me was...
I want to know more about...
Right now I'm feeling...
This experience might have been more valuable to me if...

Having said all of the above, let me unequivocally state that nothing provides greater evidence or testimony to the power of this model than the demonstrations of student understanding and skill through public performance. As soon as you are comfortable – and this is typically more a function of teacher confidence than student capacity – invite

people to your classroom to see your students in action. Once students have become accustomed to presenting their challenge results to you and their peers within the classroom, it is important to 'up the challenge' and ask them to present to people from outside the classroom.

Perhaps you may want to start with an audience of younger students, or invite a review panel of friendly teachers. Eventually, however, you need to bring in more neutral observers from outside the classroom. Invite school personnel, parents, adult friends of your students, local business people, or community leaders.*

* See Rick Lee's description of the scenario challenge panel (page 107).

* See the subsection on 'The meaningful context' (page 49).

By inviting these people into your classroom to see your students at work, you send out several important messages about the expectations you have for your students and your own professionalism as an educator. To the students, you are saying that their work is serious, that it is connected to the world outside of school,* and that adults in the community are truly interested in what they are doing. To the panel members, you are letting them know that you and your students expect to be accountable in some authentic way for your work and that you are willing to take the kind of feedback that is a normal part of adult life. And finally, for all members of your school you are modelling your willingness to 'let go' of the total teacher control that is characteristic of most traditional pedagogy* for the sake of giving your students a powerful learning experience as part of the larger community.

* See Pete Fox's description of the difficulty he had in abandoning his role as the 'Grand Lecturer' (page 69).

In addition to all the educational benefits of panel presentations, public exhibitions of student learning serve an important political function as well. When you ask parents, school staff and community members to participate in the life of your classroom you are building a political constituency.

Every person who sees your students in action is one more person who has first-hand information about what is really happening in your classroom. We all know how rumours and unfounded gossip sprout like weeds when someone tries something out of the norm in a school. If you want to bring your CSP garden to full flower, you need the help of many hands to uproot those weeds before they strangle your efforts. Consider these political implications when you invite people to your classroom as observers or panel members.

2. CSP in Your School: Greenhouse or Gobi? Advice for Senior Managers*

Introduction

* Bruce Bonney and Matt Murray – formerly Principal, now Superintendent at Gilboa-Conesville Central School (see Pete Fox's vignette, page 66) – have recently designed a CSP Senior Management training institute based on the principles outlined by Bruce in this article.

CSP institutes are designed to be a hothouse of learning. During the course of our institutes, we try to plant and nurture the seed of CSP in each of our participants. We hope that by an institute's conclusion this seed germinates and each participant departs as a viable CSP seedling – intellectually stimulated by the experience, highly motivated to grow in their learning, and full of CSP potential. If we have succeeded, our institute graduates are ready to apply their new-found knowledge and skill at a novice level.

Unfortunately we, their CSP instructors, do not accompany our seedlings back into the world. Instead, they return to a variety of educational settings where they are under the stewardship of their senior management and the influence of their colleagues. The probability of their survival, then, rests largely upon the quality of the environment to which they return. Knowing this, I tend to ask senior management a fairly straightforward question when they inquire about how to help CSP move forward in their schools. 'Exiting our institutes, will our CSP seedlings return to a greenhouse or to the Gobi?'

CSP Senior Manager as Master Gardener

I speak to senior managers about CSP using the imagery of the garden because long ago I came to appreciate that nurturing this model is a complex, almost mysterious process that is much more organic than mechanistic in nature. Now having said that, please note that this insight is not based upon any claim to profound horticultural expertise. Like any other amateur soil sifter, I've had more than my fair share of brown leaves and shrivelled plants to show for my efforts. Nonetheless, I have learned over time that if I attend to the fundamentals of good gardening practice and create the best conditions possible for nurturing my plants and flowers, generally speaking, I get decent results. The same holds true for supporting the growth of staff in their new CSP learning.

We cannot coerce our carrots

One of the first things I had to learn as a gardener was that I cannot coerce my carrots! While I consistently strive to perform all the mechanical functions of a good gardener that may ensure a successful harvest (weeding, watering, composting, etc.), experience has reminded me that I am engaging in a process over which I have limited control. Because I want to raise a successful crop, I willingly learn and do all I can to create a healthy and nurturing environment for my seedlings. However, at the end of the day, nature will largely determine the growth rate and maturation of my plants.

* See Pete Fox's description of how the senior management at Gilboa 'helped establish among the staff the same kind of learning environment that the teachers tried to create in their classroom' (page 71).

So it is with staff returning from CSP training.* Even the most highly motivated CSP graduates will apply their learning at different rates and at varying levels of sophistication. It takes many CSP experiences and often three or more years of practice before the typical CSP teacher feels completely comfortable with this model. And even then, all of us who take this approach seriously realise that we always have something more to learn.

* The seductively cheap but largely ineffective 'cascade' model of staff development.

Senior managers who demand instant results – classrooms transformed and test scores soaring within the month – will be sadly disappointed, and in all likelihood will kill whatever chance their CSP charges have for success. So often I hear our graduates report that their line managers expect early on to observe a successful CSP lesson, or request data to show that students are achieving at higher levels, or, even worse, want them to teach their colleagues how to 'do' CSP.* None of these requests is appropriate for a novice. And, in my view, all of these demands reveal a fundamental ignorance of the learning process in general and the CSP model in particular.

Transforming Teaching & Learning

Any experienced gardener instantly recognises the absurdity of expecting a plant to flower, yield fruit, or reseed and multiply before it grows to full maturity. No plant can be forced to produce before its time. The processes of nature must take their course if a healthy result is to be realised. Why then do we expect to defy the natural processes of learning as they apply to the professional development of teachers? **CSP novice practitioners, like seedlings, need time and nurturing support to reach full maturity.**

Successful CSP managers understand this and try to think 'organic' as they work to bring in a full harvest.

Knowing your plants

While a healthy dose of patience is a prime attribute of those entrusted with the care of a CSP practitioner, experience with and understanding of the CSP classroom model is of equal importance. The CSP model is more than a collection of sound educational principles and practices. To understand the power of this model, a learner needs to engage it experientially; to *feel and do it*, not just *read and talk it*. Managers who go through an institute, therefore, discover quickly that working with this model is at least as much about having a collaborative mindset as it is about expanding their personal repertoire of management tools and techniques.*

* This comes through strongly in the vignettes in Section 3 from senior managers such as Linda Marshall (see her section on 'Future plans ...' on page 95), Brian Speedie (page 97), Anne Callan (page 101) and Rick Lee (page 105).

If there is one characteristic common to those schools where CSP has been highly successful, it is that the senior managers of those educational establishments have gone through CSP training with members of their own staff.* Senior managers send two powerful messages to their staff by attending training with them:

* 'Our superintendent and principal gave us full support... Most important, they themselves took the programme and began to conduct our staff meetings in a CSP format' (Pete Fox, page 69).

1. 'I will share in the risk of learning.'

Learning anything new is risky.* All novices make mistakes and misjudgements resulting in uncomfortable feelings or downright embarrassment. This is particularly the case in the teaching profession where for so many years we have promulgated the mythology that part of great teaching is always to know the right answer. Leaders who use CSP accept the risks of learning right alongside their staff. As such they admit that they, like their staff, do not have all the answers. This statement of vulnerability opens the door for personnel to express their own uncertainty. Risk, shared openly and equally, can make it safe for everyone to ask for help and feedback.

* As Bruce himself put it in an interview for the **Times Educational Supplement** in August 2001: 'Real learning occurs always at the edge of our comfort zone.'

Asking for assistance is not necessarily a sign of weakness in a teacher. The same holds true for senior managers.

2. 'I value who you are, what you can do, and will work with you collaboratively.'

When school leaders attend CSP training with their teaching colleagues, they go through a unique educational experience together. The atmosphere of safe yet rigorous challenge, typical of CSP training, very purposefully disrupts established habits of thought and behaviour. Senior managers and their personnel get to see each other in a different light and in very different roles. If the senior manager is secure enough to let go of an assumed position of dominance and make room for others to display their talents, situational leadership and all sorts of previously hidden strengths emerge. A wise leader will acknowledge, celebrate and develop these talents in every member of staff – strengthening the school as a result.

See, Rick Lee's comments (page 105) about 'a strong community of revitalised practitioners determined not to let these critical skills slip through our fingers...'

The institute experience is designed to infuse participants with a common language, a set of effective group management tools and techniques, and the experience of solving complex problems collaboratively under pressure. This results in participants emerging with a bond of teamwork and camaraderie that comes from successfully meeting complex challenges together.* Again, wise senior managers recognize the capacity of this 'freshly minted' problem-solving team and use its collaborative strength to good effect back at school.

Good CSP Practice

Preparing the soil

To maximize the probability of a successful harvest, any conscientious gardener prepares the soil for planting. Similarly, a senior manager who wants CSP to flourish needs to prepare the way; both to inspire interest in the training and create a safe and nurturing environment for the seedlings who return.

It is of central importance that senior managers create an interest in CSP among their staff but nevertheless allow free choice regarding training, so that those who choose to attend the training 'own' their decision to do so.

One sure way to kill any chance of a CSP harvest is to start by mandating or coercing attendance at training. I have never seen a heavy-handed, top-down approach succeed with this model. You cannot coerce quality!

Transforming Teaching & Learning

May I suggest three different strategies for creating this climate of interest:

1. As a programme, CSP recognizes the power of first-hand experience as a catalyst for powerful learning. This certainly holds true when trying to inspire the interest of teachers in the CSP classroom approach. By far the most effective way to prepare a positive reception for CSP is to send a team of highly respected, professionally mature staff members to see the model in action in someone's classroom(s).* It is difficult to deny evidence of sophisticated student understanding and developing skills when it is happening right in front of you; and this is exactly what observers in a high-quality CSP classroom will see and hear. Likewise, there are few things more convincing than the testimony of credible eyewitnesses. Please note the word 'credible' as a criterion for your witnesses. Those who go to view CSP in action and report back to their colleagues must enjoy a reputation back at school for integrity and a healthy professional scepticism if the story of their CSP experience is to have impact. Choose these observers wisely.

   * One of the aims of Level 2 CSP training is to prepare teachers to run 'open classrooms' where colleagues from their own and other schools can see the model in competent action. There have already been some striking examples in the UK of such a process leading to major commitments to CSP.

2. Send your personnel to a CSP taster or workshop conducted by an experienced CSP practitioner.* In addition to learning about the programme from a knowledgeable source, your delegates will participate in a workshop designed to 'walk the talk'. By that I mean that the presenter will use CSP strategies, tools and techniques to immerse delegates in the CSP classroom approach while they learn about it. Again, choosing who will attend such an experience and report back is an important decision.

   *Further information on 'taster' courses is available from Network Eductional Press Ltd.

3. Finally, invite an experienced CSP practitioner to come to your school to meet with interested staff. While this kind of introduction is not nearly as experiential and potentially powerful as those previously mentioned, it does provide your teachers with an opportunity to ask questions and take the measure of a colleague who has actually used the model. Obviously, if the CSP representative has a videotape to show of his/her practice or that of other CSP practitioners in action, so much the better.*

   * Barrow Community Learning Partnership (see Rick Lee's vignette, page 105) has produced an excellent video of CSP in their schools. Further information from Network Educational Press Ltd.

You will note that in all cases I recommend that your staff be introduced to the CSP model by front-line educators who have had personal experience with the model, using it with real students under real classroom conditions. Since credibility is the coin of our realm, we believe strongly in the concept of 'teachers teaching teachers'. This model is based completely on the first-hand experiences of seasoned CSP educators. In our view, they are the ones most qualified and most effective in sharing it.

Planting out in the garden

Let us assume that you have a group of staff members eager to go to a CSP institute. What can you do as a senior manager to increase the probability of receiving full value for the time and investment you expend in sending them there?

Select healthy plants

In the early days, the growth of CSP within a school is as dependent upon 'who' is associated with the effort as 'what' they are doing. It is certainly no secret that schools, like other organizations, are moved by the power and influence of personal relationships. Knowing this, it is critical that the first group of CSP seedlings transplanted back into the school environment be of very hardy stock.

In my experience, educators who do particularly well with this programme are individuals who are personally and professionally mature. They know what they can do, what they can't do, and are comfortable with who they are.

Characteristically, they have a repertoire of successful teaching practice that supports them as they manoeuvre through the uncertain times of new ideas and practices. They can accept a bit of chaos and ambiguity. They can handle the scrutiny of others. Their egos and reputations are of such substance that they can withstand the scepticism, sharp questions, and occasionally hostile response that may accompany any serious challenge to established convention.*

* Pete Fox (see page 66) is a classic example of the power of this principle. Pete's comments notwithstanding, Matt Murray's invitation to him to take CSP training on that 'fateful' day in 1992 was probably a bit more calculated than he makes out!

In short, CSP stretches the repertoire of even seasoned educators. It most definitely is not a remedial programme for teachers who are fundamentally weak. In the beginning, encourage your best to attend the training.

Consider companion planting

Trying to introduce anything new in a school is often very difficult. Trying to introduce something new by yourself is, in my experience, not only doubly difficult, but often a formula for martyrdom.

Gardeners know that certain groups of flowers and vegetables when planted together create a synergy that is incredibly beneficial to all. The same can hold true for your CSP transplants.

* Rick Lee's observations (see page 105) about 'a strong community of revitalised practitioners' strongly support this suggestion.

I strongly suggest that you send teams of educators to Level I training so that they have a common experience and vocabulary with which to support each other when they return.* Your team of CSP delegates need not actually work with the same age group or within the same academic discipline. What they do need is to be a group of educators who see themselves as a team, representing a range of strengths and talents, and committed to helping each other get through the challenges of their new learning.

Hardenoff, then support your plants

The hothouse environment of a CSP institute is designed to be safe, warm, and friendly to budding ideas and emerging practices. Transplants, fresh from this cosy setting, need time to adjust before being exposed to the full glare of public scrutiny or the chilling comments of critical colleagues or parents. Senior managers must anticipate this time of transition and provide CSP seedlings with a bubble of protection to get them through the early days.

The following are some strategies I've found helpful in this regard:

1. Senior managers should meet with their CSP graduates and debrief them regarding their institute experience. Ask questions that will help them reflect, clarify their thinking and plan their first efforts at implementation:

    ● What did you find to be most valuable to you in the institute experience?

    ● How might you use some of the principles and practices learned in your institute to modify something you already do? What are you willing to try first?

    ● How will you know if you are using some CSP ideas/practices successfully? What will the results look like/sound like?

    ● What kind of support/assistance can I provide as your senior manager?

    As part of this meeting, managers should encourage their charges to set modest expectations for themselves at first. Reassure them that it is OK to move along with small steps, trying things within their range of comfort and current repertoire. In short, provide them with the same advice, reasonable target-setting and support you would give any new learner whose success is important.*

    > *See again Pete Fox's comments about how Gilboa's senior managers 'deliberately created a safe environment in which teachers were encouraged to take risks' (page 69).

2. Provide your CSP trained personnel with time to collaborate. All CSP practitioners benefit from opportunities to reflect on their experiences with others. None of us has the range of knowledge or repertoire to deal with all the challenges of the modern classroom. It is only when we have the opportunity to work with others of similar inspiration that we get a chance to tap into the incredibly deep reservoir of diverse talent and capacity evident within a group. While contributing our measure, we also replenish the vessel of our own professionalism in the process.

3. Out of this collaboration, successful CSP schools create an internal network of support to foster professional reflection and problem-solving. Leaders within these schools realize that in the early days they will want to invite CSP experts from outside to provide their staff with valuable information, guided practice, insights and feedback. In the long run, however, they know that full implementation will only come when they develop an internal mechanism that is fundamentally self-sufficient; recycling the experience and energy of the group in ways that help everyone to grow. Giving your CSP staff the time and opportunity to work together and begin solving their own problems is a major step in that direction.*

    > *Both Brian Speedie (page 97) and Anne Callan (page 101) describe ways in which they have used the CSP model to give their colleagues such time and opportunity.

* Forrest Howie (page 75) describes how he 'spread the word' to colleagues and parents, and how his comprehensive CSP formative assessment records demonstrated the effectiveness of the programme in helping his pupils to develop 'critical skills' and 'fundamental dispositions'.

* See Anne Callan's vignette (page 101).

* 'Principles are indivisible.' See the margin note about J. Edwards Deming in Bruce's 'Staying Alive' article (page 122).

* This section should be read in conjunction with the section 'Use results to build a constituency for your approach' in 'Advice for Newly Trained Critical Skills Teachers' (pages 124–126).

4. Be very open and up front with everyone about CSP. Let staff, parents and students know that some of your teachers,* and ideally you, are learning to do things that may appear different from established norms. CSP is not a fungus that thrives in dark, damp, hidden places. It needs the fresh air of collegial conversation and sharing of ideas to grow.

    Gardens do not develop error-free. Recognize this openly and encourage others to accept that new learning involves – indeed guarantees – mistakes, mishaps and misjudgements that will require attention.* Treat all that happens regarding CSP – brilliant and not so brilliant – as experience to be processed through reflection. 'What has been going well?' and 'What might we need to reconsider or work to improve for next time?' are two questions that must be part of the mind-set of leaders who hope to succeed with CSP.

5. Finally, senior managers who are serious about moving CSP forward in their school find ways to send the message that they want to give CSP a fair chance to grow. One of the best ways of doing this is to model CSP tools and techniques in staff meetings.*

    Ask the staff to describe what a *quality professional discussion* will look like and sound like before debating some school policy or issue; then hold them to the criteria. Ask the staff to form small groups to *brainstorm and distil* ideas or strategies for solving some problem. Use a *sweep* to collect and record responses.

Not only might these approaches improve the efficiency and productivity of the meetings, they will also create a climate of expectation that problems will be addressed collaboratively, formal structures will be used to guide group interaction, and criteria will be identified up front to help ensure quality work – all characteristics of a CSP classroom environment.

From this discussion one major insight should emerge. Virtually all of the strategies a teacher might use to create a classroom environment that supports high-quality, collaborative problem-solving are equally valid for a senior manager when seeking the same result with staff.*

Care and feeding*

Quality feedback is vital to growth! More than anything else, new CSP people need appropriate doses of quality feedback, judiciously applied. Feedback, of course, includes the whole range of response and information we receive that contributes to our sense of 'How am I doing?' All of us know the feeling we get when blind-sided by raw feedback coming from a disgruntled student, parent or associate. In the heat of a moment, strident words and intemperate accusations are sometimes cast directly into our face.

Taken aback, defences up, we emotionally if not physically recoil. Most often we respond by trying to protect, explain or justify ourselves. Rarely are we prepared to hear, much less consider, the important truth that may or may not lie buried within the emotional exchange. Like the blowing leaves, grass clippings, animal droppings, bits of paper and lost buttons that may litter a garden, feedback can come in from any source at any time – whether invited or not. Clearly, not all feedback is appreciated, or welcome. **Quality feedback, on the other hand, is of a different order.**

Quality feedback is like compost; the remarkable 'black gold' that, when applied to plants, serves to protect, feed and invigorate growth throughout the garden.

To become compost, however, raw organic materials must be piled off to the side in some enclosure (ideally well aerated and moistened occasionally) to lie quiet for a spell. Over time the processes of nature work to break these materials down into their basic elements, neutralizing the harmful and reconstituting the remaining material into a form that may be reintroduced into the cycle of life to great benefit.

It is virtually the same with quality feedback. Here, however, it is the raw data of experience and observation that accumulates in the brain of the observer. There, with time and reflection, the data are transformed into coherent statements of insight and advice; nutrients now ready to be returned to the cycle of learning to the benefit of all.

Permit me to share, therefore, some things a senior manager might want to consider when offering quality feedback:*

➡ High-quality feedback is the product of considered judgement borne of careful observation and reflection over time. Senior managers who want to give teachers quality feedback regarding CSP will find ways to observe their colleagues over a period of time. Ideally, they will look for patterns of behaviour upon which to base their conclusions rather than one or two isolated – possibly aberrational – incidents. It is also extremely helpful if the one providing the feedback can support general statements with very specific examples or observations that illustrate or support the conclusion under discussion.

➡ High-quality feedback is best offered when the recipient is ready to hear it. In most instances where I have given feedback to someone, I've been most successful when the recipient knows it is coming. Indeed, it is best when I've gained their consent by saying something like, 'I've got some feedback to share with you. Could we find some time to talk?' This gives the recipient some measure of control over the situation that may make the conversation less threatening. It also gives them an opportunity to prepare emotionally for the discussion.

* The **Level 1 CSP Coaching Manual** has a particularly insightful section on 'Feedback and Assessment', including the following statement: 'Feedback is critical to the learning process, especially when behaviours are being learned. We look to our environment constantly for clues about how well we are doing. If that feedback is readily available and unambiguous, we can internalise our needs and make corrections, or we can acknowledge our successes and press on to something new.' This advice is equally applicable to the relationship between senior managers and teachers as between teachers and pupils.

➡ High-quality feedback is timely, but rarely instantaneous. I have coached competitive sports teams for many years in my career as an educator. Virtually all of the ill-considered comments I regret were statements made in a moment of high emotion during and/or just after a contest or match. I have found it impossible to be at once a high-quality participant in and dispassionate observer of an event. For that reason, I learned never to make substantive pronouncements about my team or individual performances until I had a chance to back off from the moment and regain my balance and perspective. While this may not be practical advice for all occasions, I do believe it is sound as a general principle.

➡ Make sure both sides in the conversation understand the criteria used to guide the feedback. Before delegates in our Level I CSP training leave, we ask them to write out the criteria they would like an informed observer to use when observing their classroom to see their work with CSP. Along with the production of this document, we encourage the delegates to have a conversation with their line managers to discuss what they've written. This dialogue is intended to help the manager know what to 'look for/listen for' as evidence of the teacher's implementation of CSP principles and practices as a novice.* For the manager's part, I suggest you take the initiative to engage in this conversation and ask, 'What do you want me to look for or listen for as evidence of your novice implementation of the CSP model?' Agreeing on these criteria and using them as the guidelines for feedback regarding the classroom observation should help things go well.

*Note the similarity between this process and the use of anecdotal evidence as described by John Kerr (page 60).

➡ High-quality feedback is contextualized to the recipient and their needs. To thrive, some plants must stand tall, prominently exposed to the full glare of constant sunlight. Others find such exposure withering, doing much better in dappled sunlight or in the shade of more prominent species. Likewise, some organisms must be watered and fed regularly while others can get along quite nicely with very little attention. The wise gardener and manager knows his/her plants well and adjusts both the style and substance of their care and feeding accordingly.

Sharing the harvest

One of the great joys of CSP is the opportunity to watch students produce results that are clear evidence of developing knowledge and skill. Through the struggle to meet CSP challenges, students strengthen their capacity to solve problems, overcome adversity, and grapple with the uncertainty that is so characteristic of modern life. It is crucial that senior managers encourage their staff to share the evidence of student learning with the public.

Share the learning with the public

As soon as possible, CSP teachers should ask their students to present their challenges before panels of 'judges' who will give them open and appropriately direct feedback regarding the quality of their work.

Initially these panels might be composed of friendly and familiar faces, usually from within the school, who will view student efforts with a sympathetic eye. In time, however, membership on challenge review panels should come from informed members of the public who will give students increasingly 'authentic' feedback resembling that which adults would receive under similar conditions in the 'real' world.*

> * Co-opting local business managers onto such panels can bring a number of benefits – not least by confirming that the skills and attitudes that the pupils are developing are highly relevant to the world of work.

I cannot overemphasize the value and power of these panel review experiences for students. Granted, there is risk involved, as there is with any public performance. Nonetheless, the rewards in terms of student learning, motivation, satisfaction, confidence and personal growth are well worth the effort. **All of this is true for CSP staff as well.**

Sports coaches, instructors of drama, orchestra conductors and art teachers, to name a few, all understand the anxiety and thrill of having their students perform in public. Relinquishing direct control so students can 'play the game' on their own is a scary feeling. Yet the experience of demonstrating one's knowledge and skill publicly is crucial if our students are to move to full maturity. I believe the same can be said for the teacher. Both the teacher and the students benefit tremendously from knowing, in authentic terms, how 'we' are doing. CSP training puts this experience within the grasp of any competent educator.

'WE' more than 'ME'

As a final recommendation to senior managers, let me suggest you look closely at the words 'WE' and 'ME'. If you cut out a cardboard silhouette in block letters of either of these words, you can invert it to reveal the other. I am sure many people more clever than I have discovered this on their own and used it to good effect. In any event, I quite proudly figured this out about twenty years ago while coaching one of my basketball teams. At opportune moments throughout the season, I would get out my cardboard silhouette and ask the team: 'How are we playing/working today? Are you in this for 'ME' or 'WE'?' This turned out to be a wonderful way to focus my players' attention on their individual conduct and its impact on our collaborative success. It led to some very interesting and insightful discussions. Naturally, once introduced to CSP, I used this technique there as well.

I mention this not only as an idea to pass on or even use with your staff, but as a guide to your own efforts at collaborative leadership. As I hope I have made clear, modelling desired behaviour and attitudes is an extremely powerful tool for learning.* Using 'WE' more than 'ME' language as a leader with your staff, in your classroom, or with your team is an important way to both model and contribute to the collaborative ethos you hope to develop.

Whenever praise or credit is somehow associated with the CSP work of students or staff, I suggest you make every effort to use the kind of 'WE' language that will permit everyone to share in the bounty of the harvest.

* Matt Murray (see the margin note at the beginning of this article) talks of the need for a headteacher to be a role model to staff. And in the **CSP Level 1 Training Manual**, Bruce's colleague Jack Drury writes: 'I cannot do one thing while expecting students (or staff!) to do the opposite. One of my favourite quotes is by Robert Fulghum: "Don't worry that your children don't listen to you. Worry that they are watching everything you do." '

3. Frequently Asked Questions

Over the years, hundreds of teachers have asked me dozens of questions about the principles and practice of CSP. Some issues crop up with great regularity, so I have prepared a set of considered answers to these 'frequently asked questions'. I hope that you will find them of help in your journey of self-discovery with CSP.

I have grouped these issues under the following themes:

1. grouping students
2. setting standards
3. nurturing a collaborative classroom culture.

Theme 1: Grouping students in a CSP classroom

Question 1: When should students work in groups?

By far the first consideration in addressing the issue of grouping is to determine whether you really need a group to do the task or challenge. Few things undermine the authenticity of CSP more than requiring students to work in small groups when there is no legitimate reason to do so. If you can imagine one capable student meeting the parameters of the task or challenge with reasonable quality, then you need to rethink the design of the challenge. In CSP we place students in groups because the challenge requires the diverse capacities of more than one person to engage it successfully. There must be meaningful work for everyone in the group. If there isn't, do not put students in a group!

Question 2: What is the best size of group for CSP work?

Fit group size to the complexity of the task and the experience level of your students and you. In the beginning of the year, I recommend you keep group size small – pairs or groups of three at most. This size of group permits both you and your students to begin your exploration of CSP at a lower level of risk. For you, a challenge designed for two or three should be fairly simple, directed towards reasonably straightforward outcomes, and involve a time-frame that is acceptably brief. For students, a group of two or three gives them the opportunity to develop skill with CSP group process techniques (Task roles, *brainstorm and distillation, sweep,* etc.) while learning to handle the personality and social issues engendered by a limited number of people. When you are prepared to design challenges of greater complexity, and your students are ready to work productively with more people, then by all means increase the size of your groups.

Question 3: What is the best way to organise group membership?

Choose a grouping mechanism that fits your desired outcomes. Basically I know of only four different ways to arrive at group membership. I have used all of these strategies at various times and will comment on each as I list them.

1. Teacher arranges the groups
This approach gives the teacher some measure of control in balancing student strengths among the groups and perhaps a chance to be proactive regarding the teaming of 'difficult' students together. There are many published resources regarding co-operative learning theory that describe methods of forming this kind of group.*

* See, for example, the **CSP Level 1 Coaching Kit**, page 122; and 'How to Begin' (page 25) in **Cooperative Learning** by Grisham and Molinelli. (See bibliography).

I used this approach extensively my first year with CSP and despite early resistance from some students, it worked well, provided I kept the students in this configuration long enough (at least through three or four challenges) for them to adjust to each other and 'bond'.

The main disadvantage of this mechanism is that the students do not 'own' the choice of group membership and therefore find it convenient to blame the teacher for any group dysfunction. Any teacher using this approach with challenging students must be prepared to 'stay the course' with the group assignments and outlast student complaints.

2. Students arrange the groups
As a teacher, I found that this was the most challenging way of choosing groups – for a time. Unsurprisingly, less responsible students exploited the opportunity to team with their mates and wasted all sorts of time. Frequently, they would leave some classmates out of the group formation process as well.

Anticipating these difficulties, I learned to design several simple and very brief challenges for groups forming this way. As part of each one, I insisted that ALL students be included in a group. Additionally, I was adamant that all criteria for quality be fulfilled. Finally, in the debriefing of each challenge I always asked the question: 'Do you feel the grouping of your team has had any impact on the quality of your work?'*

* See also Question 12 on page 151.

Predictably, some students denied there was any connection. Eventually, however, one student would break the code of silence and admit that sometimes working just with one's friends was not the best strategy for producing quality work. When other students in the class acknowledged the truth of the statement, I knew we had moved to a higher level of honesty and maturity within the class. We could then move on and honestly discuss the reasons for group work and how each challenge was an opportunity for each student to accept responsibility for his/her own behaviour and learning, and to demonstrate his/her increasing maturity, knowledge of content and collaborative skill.

As I became more comfortable with CSP over the years, I deliberately started each year with students choosing their own groups so that we could get at these issues early on. It wasn't an easy strategy, but over time it yielded great dividends.

Transforming Teaching & Learning

3. Groups are formed at random

Each year I would tell my students on the first day of class: 'One of my expectations for each of you this year is that before our time together is over, you will demonstrate your capacity to work productively with every other student in this class.' In schools where CSP has been highly successful over a period of years, this expectation is system-wide and random grouping is the norm in all CSP classes.

Random grouping is a clear expression of a teacher's faith that the students are capable of quality group work and learning under most any circumstance. For the students, comfort with random grouping usually indicates that they are ready to focus directly on the criteria for success rather than be distracted constantly by the personalities of team members.

When both teacher and students are satisfied that high-quality work and learning can result within random groups, it is an indicator that the sense of community within the classroom is exceptionally strong.

4. Groups are set by matching talents with jobs (Job/Talent Matrix)

Teachers who want to use this method of grouping will ask their students to help identify those specific talents or capacities necessary to complete the specified challenge successfully. They will then draw a chart (matrix) listing these capacities along a vertical axis as jobs or task roles to be played in each team.

Then, the students and teacher will recognize those in the class who have these special talents. The names of these students are entered along the horizontal axis of the chart. Finally, teacher and students match the entries on the horizontal and vertical axes to ensure that these talents are distributed fairly among the teams.

In short, grouping is done with the requirements of the task and best interests of each team in mind, rather than the personal preferences of either the students or the teacher.

Success with this approach, much like random grouping, is a clear indicator of a healthy community within the classroom. This grouping strategy also highlights the advantages of heterogeneity in a CSP classroom. Like any biome, a vigorous classroom community requires a healthy assortment of very diverse organisms.*

* Notice how this approach turns the common argument against 'mixed ability' grouping on its head!

Successful collaborative problem-solving depends on the contributions of a wide range of talents. That does not necessarily mean that all individuals within the system are equally strong or equally healthy in all areas. It does mean that the mix of individuals is sufficiently diverse to provide the talents and strengths necessary for successful problem-solving.

A CSP teacher can make the desirability of heterogeneity quite visible to all by designing challenges that require talents or capacities not commonly considered assets in the course of normal schoolwork. Ask your students to do challenges requiring that

* A classic example of the powerful way in which CSP challenges take account of Gardner's multiple intelligence theory. See also the annotated challenge on page 45.

they dance, sing, sew costumes, build something, draw, write poetry, fix or invent a machine, play or compose music.* See what happens to the social value of students with these talents as their classmates seek them out as team members.

Using the Job/Talent Matrix to determine groups in such challenges gives students with unique talents a chance to see their full value recognized in front of everyone.

Theme 2: Setting standards for students' work

Question 4: Why is it important to set standards for 'product' *and* 'process'?

The CSP classroom is a comprehensive approach to teaching and learning. Whereas curricular content may be the primary focus in other classrooms, in a CSP classroom we challenge students to master content while simultaneously achieving progress in two other related areas of learning. In CSP we look to:

➡ create a 'quality' classroom community environment that is emotionally and physically safe for all students and supportive of learning through collaborative work

➡ engage students in complex, relatively open-ended problems-to-solve (challenges) that produce evidence of increasingly sophisticated understanding of curricular content

➡ develop in students a range of specific skills we know are 'critical' to success in school and life thereafter.

Achieving all of these at once is an ambitious undertaking. Yet many CSP practitioners realize these ends on a fairly regular basis and are able to verify that they are doing so. How?

Successful CSP practitioners set *quality criteria* and assess student performance in terms of these criteria as a matter of course in their classrooms. By that I mean that they and their students regularly spend time discussing expectations for the products they create, the group processes they will use, and skills they will develop. And, most important, they assess their progress in each area using these criteria.

Questions 5–7 consider each of the areas cited above and see how we might set standards – that is *quality criteria** – that will permit everyone involved to have a clear picture regarding the quality of their performance.

* See, 'The Pupil Cycle' on pages 51–57.

Question 5: How do we set standards for the processes of a collaborative classroom community?

Many students come to CSP-trained teachers after years of classroom experience in which they were expected to sit down, be quiet, and regurgitate information that the teacher has told them is important. In such a setting, it is not unusual for students to go through an entire year without having either worked with other students in the room or got to know them well personally. And why should they? *If the essential relationship in the class is between the individual student and the teacher and any communication among students is regarded as socializing, messing around or cheating, then why should a student be concerned about, or learn to work with, other students?**

* The DfES' **A Strategy to 2006** (2002) states: 'Our objectives are to … enable all young people to … equip themselves with the skills … and personal qualities needed for life and work' (see page 158). It is difficult to see how they can do this if communications with each other in the classroom are regarded as 'messing around'!

Students with this kind of school experience are sometimes shocked when they arrive in your CSP classroom. This is especially the case when you speak of a 'classroom community' and the challenges you place before them require that they deal with each other. While they may have the capacity to be a good team-mate and produce high-quality performances on the athletic field, on stage, or in the orchestra, and so on, they don't yet know how to behave as members of a classroom community. Nor do they know how to produce high-quality collaborative work in an academic context. Regardless of their age, most of your students may be complete novices at collaborative academic work. You are going to have to teach them! How?

Following are some suggestions:

1. Recall your institute experience as a model and mimic its processes appropriately in your classroom

In your Level 1 institute training you no doubt had a small group discussion very early on in which you were asked to describe what your instructors should 'look for and listen for' as evidence that you and your team-mates were having a *quality discussion*. In that same activity I am sure one of you functioned as 'group facilitator', another as 'group recorder', and perhaps yet another as a 'timekeeper'. You were then asked to *brainstorm and distil* your ideas on the question. Finally, you reported your thinking to the whole group using a *sweep.**

* See 'quality discussion standards' on pages 38–40.

This portion of the institute was designed to help you learn some group processes (*quality discussion, brainstorm, distil, sweep*) and task roles (facilitator, recorder and timekeeper) that are fundamental to productive group interaction. I am confident that your instructors took some time to describe the expectations for each task role and group process as you used them. And, of course, you had the opportunity to practise each of them with the instructors' guidance as you addressed the question about a *quality discussion*.

This, in microcosm, is a series of steps you might use in your classroom to introduce your students to the processes and roles they will need to master as they work towards collaboration. Note that in every case, your instructors helped you to *identify* the process or role; *describe* what it will 'look like and sound like' when executed properly; *model* its use if necessary; then *practise* it in some authentic context. Finally, of course, the instructors offered *feedback* on the performance to guide the 'next steps' towards improvement.

You can see from this sequence that agreeing on the *quality criteria* in terms of *specific observable behaviours* to 'look for and listen for' is absolutely essential to both the teaching and the assessment of the learning. If we don't know 'upfront' what it is we are trying to achieve in language we all can understand, only students who are highly intuitive or those with previous experience will be able to move towards the desired end with confidence and purpose.

2. *Think through those group processes or roles you will need for success in your classroom*

Then ask the students to help you form quality criteria for each of them as early in the year as possible. Do you want your students to be a *quality audience* whenever someone in the class is speaking? Do you want them to know what it means to be a *quality group member*? Should they consider the difference between being a 'boss' and being a 'leader' of a group? If so, I suggest you follow a process similar to the one described in 1 above, so that your expectations are made visible and real for all students.

Asking your students to help you describe what to 'look for and listen for' as quality criteria is a process that can be applied to any group process or role you want your students to master.

3. *Be prepared to break down the desired group process or role into its simplest and most fundamental 'look for and listen for' components*

Remember that some of your students may have absolutely no life experience with civil or productive social interaction. For instance, while introducing the concept of a *quality discussion* to his students, one of my colleagues had to list the following criteria:

- (i)   your desks will touch each other
- (ii)   you will face each other
- (iii) you will permit the speaker to finish his/her statements without interruption.

If your students have never seen the process or role before, you may have to serve as their first model.

Question 6: How do we set standards to get quality *products* in challenges?

Among some educators, problem-based learning has a sullied reputation because individual students participating in group projects often come away with little understanding of the intended content. For example, let us imagine a teacher wants a small group of students to create a map reflecting their understanding of the impact of World War I on the political boundaries of certain countries in Europe. Among her criteria for success she mentions that:

- (i)   the map must accurately reflect the boundaries of the countries before and after WWI
- (ii)   the map must be interesting, colourful and easy to read
- (iii) all names and places on the map must be spelled correctly
- (iv) the map must have a key with symbols identified correctly.

Transforming Teaching & Learning

As a result of this challenge, our teacher gets a wall full of beautifully reproduced maps that meet the criteria as listed. Yet, when she asks her students about their work, it is clear very few have any real understanding of what the maps mean in terms of the content she intended. Let's see how this situation might be addressed:

1. Recognize that all criteria are not created equal!

Distinguish among the kinds of criteria you require and consider how each will or will not contribute to realizing the desired outcome of the challenge. If we look at the criteria listed above, it is obvious that most of the requirements are directed at the 'FORM' of the map (i.e. the way the product is put together, arranged, presented – see criteria (ii), (iii) and (iv)).

Form criteria are important to specify because they help students understand the importance of quality with regard to the *medium* through which they communicate their understanding. If an observer can't read the map, or interpret the key, or the places and names are misidentified or misspelled, then clearly the quality of the communication suffers.

By the same token, however, a student can meet *all* of the form criteria as written and not have a clue about the 'SUBSTANCE' or 'CONTENT' of the map.

In short, if the standards of quality for a product do not include descriptors that specifically require some kind of 'evidence of understanding' (that is, **content** criteria), then a student can create acceptable product in terms of form and still not know anything of importance about the content of the challenge.

So, how could the criteria for success be modified so that some 'evidence of understanding' is produced?

First, require that the map contain 'annotations' describing and/or explaining the implications of the changed boundaries for certain ethnic populations within Europe, or some other focal question. Moreover, require that each group member contribute at least one of these annotations to the map. This raises the probability that each student will know something about at least one area of the content.

Second, require that any group member be prepared to discuss and respond appropriately to questions regarding any annotation on the map.* This raises the probability that students will share the content of the map among themselves so that everyone has some knowledge of all the intended content.

* See annotation (vii) in the annotated challenge on page 45.

---

2. Recognize that group challenges do have limitations as vehicles for assessing individual understanding

Group challenges that are well designed provide students with a great opportunity to learn many things on a variety of levels; things the teacher intended and some things not intended. That is part of the richness of the challenge experience.

The more students involved in a challenge, however, the more difficult it is to assess the level of contribution and content understanding of each of the individuals in the group. This is a function of many factors, not least of which is the inability of any observer to watch and interpret the responses of all students all the time. No matter how clearly the teacher has spelled out the content criteria, this logistical reality severely limits the value of a group challenge as a vehicle for assessing the specific level of understanding of a specific student in a specific area of content.

Understanding this limitation, experienced CSP practitioners look to other means for assessing the content understanding of individual students. Reflective essays; an exam; Socratic questioning; and 1-on-1 interviews are all approaches that experienced educators use to get a clearer picture of an individual student's level of content understanding after completing a challenge.

Question 7: How do we set standards to develop Critical Skills?

As the name CSP implies, developing life-long skills in our students while they master content is a very important piece of what we do. Indeed, many of us would say that targeting a skill to work on at the same time that we are mastering some portion of the curriculum is *the* distinguishing characteristic of a CSP challenge compared to other problem-based approaches.

It should come as no surprise at this point to say that the way to set standards for developing a specific skill associated with a challenge is similar to that cited above for a group process or quality product.

In all cases, the key activity is to engage your students in a conversation in which you discuss your expectations in terms of 'specific observable behaviours' that you will 'look for and listen for' as the students use the targeted skill during the challenge.

There is, however, one very specific suggestion I have for you when working to develop a *critical skill* in your students as they do a challenge: **Target only one skill and one of its performance indicators to observe at a time.**

Many novice CSP practitioners list three or four skills for their students to work on as they do a challenge. Initially this seems to make sense since virtually any complex problem-solving involves the critical skills of *problem-solving, organization, decision-making* and *creative thinking* – just to name a few. While this may technically be correct, it is also irrelevant from the standpoint of helping students actually get better in any given performance area.

For students to improve, they must focus on a limited set of targeted behaviours at one time, practise the behaviours under controlled conditions, and then get feedback from an informed observer regarding the quality of the performance. With 20–30 students in a class at a time and only one teacher/observer to function as a 'skills coach', it is manifestly impossible for a teacher to give clear and specific feedback to individual students unless the focus of the feedback is extremely narrow. Hence, 'look for and listen for' evidence of only one performance indicator of one skill at a time!

Critical Skills classrooms help students improve their group processes, academic product and life-long skills when 'quality' is a top priority for everyone. This is achieved when setting standards/criteria for quality for everything that is really important and getting feedback on them becomes a ritualized part of the life of the CSP classroom community.*

* See the subsection: 'What the teacher does: C – Feedback and Assessment' on pages 60–62.

Theme 3: Nurturing a collaborative classroom culture

Question 8: In CSP, what do you mean when you talk about a 'classroom culture'?

I remember quite clearly the look on the faces of my colleagues when at the beginning of each year we were handed the list of students attending our classes. Some of us broke into a broad smile, others bowed our heads, shaking them in dismay. We shared a common assumption: the social 'chemistry' represented by the mix of students on our class list would largely determine whether we had a relatively 'good' year or would expend endless hours struggling to motivate the moribund and control the chaotic!

Whether we like it or not, all of our classes have a 'culture' – that is, a set of expectations, norms and patterns of behaviour that govern personal interactions within the group. Most educators know by now that the best classroom environment for learning is one free from threat where students feel physically and emotionally safe to take the risk of thinking new thoughts and trying new things. Yet many teachers feel powerless to create such an environment if the traditional methods of control and coercion fail.

CSP teachers feel differently.

CSP practitioners recognize the absolute necessity of working towards a classroom culture that is safe for all learners and supportive of collaborative work. Moreover, their training gives them a beginner's repertoire to address this goal – by design.

Question 9: Why do we need to go beyond 'getting-to-know-you' activities when we build a community?

In the beginning, novice CSP teachers mimic many of the 'getting-to-know-you' type icebreaker activities they experienced in their CSP institute. This is our hope. We know these games and activities are relatively low-risk and provide most everyone with the beginnings of a 'common ground' of interpersonal knowledge and familiarity that helps students and teacher alike to feel more aware of and comfortable with the people around them. Setting up this base of common knowledge, however, is only the beginning of building and maintaining the kind of classroom community necessary for truly collaborative work.

It is important to keep in mind that a 'classroom community' is not an end in itself. The reason we take the time and energy to develop and maintain our community is that this complex network of interpersonal relationships, growing out of the feelings, beliefs and behaviours of each individual, is the organic structure that either will or will not sustain us all through the challenges of living and learning together.

Life in a CSP classroom is oftentimes very hard work – intellectually, physically, emotionally and socially. No one, including the teacher, has the personal reservoir of intellectual, emotional or physical resources to 'make it happen' by themselves. A successful CSP environment requires the willing contribution of everyone. Everyone, therefore, needs to be invited, included, encouraged and recognized for their participation in the common endeavour. This requires a conscious 'investment' of time and energy – initially from the teacher, thereafter from the students – to develop and maintain the optimum state of good health in the classroom over time.

Science teaches us that any 'system' requires regular infusions of fresh energy to offset the natural tendency towards atrophy and chaos. So it is with your classroom community. To keep your community fit, you need to develop and maintain it throughout the year. Some important strategies to achieve this are:

→ making the health of your classroom community an overt priority (Question 10)

→ teaching the behaviours you expect in your students by modelling them yourself (Question 11)

→ making the growth and strength of the community 'visible' (Question 12)

→ using rituals and traditions to institutionalize desirable patterns (Question 13).

Question 10: How can I make the culture of my classroom a 'priority' issue with my students?

When you first mention the idea of a 'classroom community' to your students, you may find yourself looking out upon a sea of faces that is perfectly calm – without a ripple of comprehension. Do not be surprised or necessarily dismayed. Many students have never experienced a classroom in which the quality of social and emotional aspects of the learning environment was an issue for discussion. Part of your task as a CSP teacher, therefore, is to make the health of the classroom community a priority deserving of its fair share of attention.

On Day 1 of my own CSP classrooms (students aged 13–18), I extended two verbal challenges to my students:

1. 'Before our time together is over, I expect every one of you in this class to demonstrate beyond a doubt that you have worked productively with every other member of this class – and I want that to be documented.

2. 'Some time shortly after the mid-point of our term, I want to be able to confidently write a note to any supply teacher stating, "This class runs itself! Please observe and record what these students do during the class period and leave your observations for my inspection." '

Making these statements within the first 15 minutes of our first class together got my students' attention straight away. Many blanched, some moaned, others snickered. Their initial shock and scepticism was both predictable and irrelevant!

By design, I wanted my students to know that in this CSP classroom, our mission was about more than absorbing information and passing exams. I wanted them to know 'up front' that success would be measured not only by individual test scores, but by the quality of our interpersonal working relationships and our capacity to function effectively and efficiently as a team of problem-solvers.

I supported this initial conversation with my students by sending a letter home to their parents. In this, I introduced myself and described the usual outline of academic requirements of the class. The bulk of the letter, however, was devoted to an explanation of the unique aspects of our CSP classroom; the importance of building a classroom community supportive of collaboration; my goal of balancing the mastery of content with the development of student skills and attitudes that would serve their children in school and beyond; and, finally, my commitment to using 'challenges' and collaborative problem-solving as a vehicle for connecting our course content to the larger world outside of school.

Admittedly, my messages about life in our CSP classroom were not always received with universal acclaim. Nonetheless, virtually everyone – students and parents alike – appreciated early on that our CSP classroom would be different from others they had experienced. And, more important, they could see from the time I was investing in its construction, that building a healthy classroom environment in which everyone knew the expectations was a top priority.

Question 11: What do CSP teachers mean when they say it is important to 'walk the talk' with this model?

'Walking the talk' is a mantra anyone involved with CSP hears often and in many different contexts. So it is that 'walking the talk' has application for teachers who want to maintain their classroom community.

As you ask your students to consider what to 'look for and listen for' in a *quality discussion, quality audience* or *quality feedback*, be sure to consider the implications for yourself. Are you prepared to personally model and adhere to the 'specific observable behaviours' described? This is a crucially important question for any educator who takes this classroom approach seriously.*

Surely you recognize that a student will eventually call you to task on a perceived or real infraction of the standards the class sets for appropriate social interaction. How will you handle that situation?

In this regard, there is one area of teacher behaviour that we need to address straight away – *sarcasm and 'put-downs'*. More than any other behaviour, the constant use of sarcasm and its close cousins, 'put-downs', have the potential to undermine and ultimately destroy any effort to build a lasting spirit of community in the classroom.*

Sarcasm and 'put-downs' are particularly insidious for two reasons. Firstly, they are so commonly accepted among educators as a seemingly harmless weapon in our arsenal of class control; and secondly, they can be so satisfying to the perpetrator.

Before my exposure to CSP I regularly used sarcasm and sometimes 'put-downs', as did many of my colleagues. I have come to believe that my experience is not unusual. I have rarely visited a school for long without hearing sarcasm and/or 'put-downs' come into play in some fashion – either with students or among teachers themselves.

I assume that most of us think that using these devices to express our discontent, frustration, even anger with a student, is a perfectly legitimate means of asserting our position of dominance and control over students by verbally putting them 'in their place'. Sarcasm and 'put-downs' have the attraction of gaining compliance without resorting to more overt forms of coercion. From this perspective we have rationalized that they constitute a kinder and more gentle form of discipline than the more draconian measures at hand.

Moreover, sarcasm and 'put-downs' can be fun and entertaining. Frequently delivered in the guise of humour or wit, sarcasm in particular is considered a performance art in some schools and organizations. Listen to the giggles of delight coming from amused spectators as they watch some defenceless victim wither under the assault of a particularly witty teacher, and you know what I mean. The same holds true in the staffroom.

* 'If I could go back and redo the training for Gilboa teachers after all these years, there is one change I would make. I would assert over and over again that the teacher is a member of the community of learners in the classroom' (Pete Fox, quoted in **Leading the Learning School**, page 116).

* It is arguable, for example, that the major reason for the success of Pink Floyd's blockbusting 'Just Another Brick in the Wall' was due to the way young people could identify with phrases such as 'No dark sarcasm in the classroom; Teacher leave those kids alone!'

Transforming Teaching & Learning

My point here is not that any educator involved with CSP must immediately eschew all forms of sarcasm/'put-downs'. It isn't going to happen, particularly because its use is so embedded in our culture and in some organizations is interpreted as a means of displaying friendship and affection. I will suggest, however, that a CSP practitioner needs to be mindful of the impact of sarcasm and 'put-downs'.

Like the small pebbles on the motorway that fly up and dent and ding our new car, sarcasm and 'put-downs' wear away at the protective coating of mutual respect that shields individuals within the community from unnecessary emotional harm. No one pebble destroys the finish of the car. Neither does any one particular comment wreck a community.

Nonetheless, repeated over time, the sum of the damage mounts. Creating many small cracks and fissures that permit more powerful forces of corrosion to begin their work, sarcasm and 'put-downs' weaken the 'safety' of the classroom community and compromise the feeling of trust that holds it together.

CSP practitioners need to be mindful of their role in this process.

Question 12: How can I make my students more aware of the role their individual and collective behaviour plays in the health of our classroom community?

As with any learning, it is always helpful to get feedback regarding the question, 'How am I/we doing?' You and your students will benefit from feedback regarding the strength and well-being of your classroom community in the same way.

By far the easiest and most direct way of assessing the development of your classroom culture is to debrief experiences in terms of community issues. When you finish a challenge or emerge from a particularly interesting or intense classroom experience, ask your students to think about it in terms of their relationships.* You might ask questions like:

➡ During this experience, how did we treat each other? Did you all feel safe?

➡ Did the way we treated each other have an impact on the quality/outcome of this experience?

➡ What might we do differently next time?

➡ If we were going through this challenge/experience again, what would we 'look for/listen for' as evidence that we were maintaining our sense of community throughout?

*See Jo Morrison's description of how she used the 'debrief' phase of the experiential cycle to 'hold up a mirror to my students (which) provided a vehicle through which (they) examined their own behaviour and contribution to their groups' (page 112).

Another way to focus on community issues is to play games or do 'initiatives' with your students that require a high degree of co-operation. Games like those you encountered in your institute (for example 'Ball Toss') while 'safe', nevertheless put all participants into a situation where pressure, varying levels of competitive spirit, and feelings of personal comfort and competence stress the social bonds linking individuals to each other.

The 'natural' tendencies and personal qualities of individuals within the class usually reveal themselves rather quickly under such circumstances. A skilful debriefing – perhaps using the *IP3 debriefing tool**– will help participants think through the implications of the game and permit them to get those issues that create tension out in the open for discussion and resolution.

*See page 47.

Once your class – or staff – has reflected upon several experiences and begins seeing patterns in their own behaviour, you might ask them the questions:

➡ How do we know when we are functioning well as a community and when not?

➡ What do the various levels of our performance 'look like/sound like'?

* Such developmental rubrics are a uniquely powerful way of promoting effective formative assessment. They form a major focus of Level 2 CSP training.

The subsequent conversation can then be transposed into a formal 'rubric' that describes in accurate detail what each level of community performance 'looks like and sounds like' when it is occurring.* Constructing this can be a powerful exercise for developing individual and collective self-awareness. And, of course, it is infinitely useful as a referent for giving a class instant feedback on their behaviour at any given moment.

Question 13: How can I make sure the behaviours I want to see in my students become embedded in my classroom – whether I am there or not?

* See, for example, Anne Callan's vignette (page 104).

All cultures around the world find ways of institutionalizing the kinds of behaviours deemed important. I know of several teachers who use a special hand signal or some other prompt to accompany their request for a *quality audience* from their students. They report that 'like magic' the students respond and give the teacher and each other full attention.* This is a good example of a classroom community 'ritual' that supports and reinforces desired patterns of behaviour. There are many other possibilities.

* 'Check-in' has many similarities to the well known 'Circle Time'. It can also be a valuable way of finding out any areas of recent work that pupils in general may be having difficulty with.

Start off the class period or day with a 'circle-up' or 'check-in' to find out how everyone is doing emotionally.* This need not be as lengthy as those you may have experienced in your institute. Indeed, with older students it is quite possible to circle-up and do a quick sweep of the group or use a *thumb tool* to indicate if everyone is OK. That leaves a minute or two for any one individual who needs time to tell the group something important they have to share. When dealing with younger students, I have seen teachers limit a morning check-in to only four or five children on a given day. Each day of the week a different cluster or table of kids gets to share their thoughts.

Yet another ritual I have seen used with great effect at all grade levels involves the class appointing or electing 'community ambassadors'. These ambassadors answer the classroom door and quickly interview anyone coming to the room to ascertain their identity and need. The students then act on the need as appropriate. By taking on this responsibility the students learn basic interview skills, exercise judgement, save the teacher and the class from constant interruption, and act as representatives of the whole class. If the ambassadors ascertain that the visitor intends to observe the class or needs the attention of the class for some reason, they bring the visitor into the classroom, ask for a *quality audience*, introduce the visitor to the class by name, and state their business. Having experienced this process as a visitor to a number of CSP classrooms, I will tell you it is an extremely pleasant, smooth and impressive way to join a classroom without causing undue disruption.

Finally, I want to suggest very strongly that you find ways to integrate CSP student alumni back into your classroom. Use former students as challenge review panel members, as mentors, as guest speakers, or as 'guides' to your CSP classroom at the beginning of each year. The students who return to your classroom immediately feel very special and more often than not will tell the current generation of students just how lucky they are to be in your class. In effect, you are inviting them to play the role of community 'elder' as one who has special knowledge, insight and wisdom regarding the inner workings of the CSP classroom culture. Do not underestimate the power this image may have for your graduates. It may be one of the few times in their lives they have been recognized and honoured in such an authentic way. At the same time, this symbolic 'passing of the torch' sends a powerful message to the new generation as well. Clearly it tells them that there is substance to this idea of a 'community', that what goes on in your classroom has great value to other students, and that they have a responsibility to create a worthy legacy as well.

Both the rituals and traditions help CSP students understand that membership in a classroom community is very special. Within the community they can find the acceptance, support and feeling of 'belonging' that is so important to all of us.

National Educational Initiatives and CSP
Jo Morrison

**Education and Skills:
Delivering Results**

A Strategy to 2006

'... enable all young
people to ... equip
themselves with the
skills, knowledge and
personal qualities
needed for life and
work.'

**Education Bill
2001**

'... we want to free
schools to develop the
ideas that will raise
standards.'

**14–19 Extending
Oportunities, Raising
Standards**

'Young people must be
prepared for an adult
life in which they are
involved as active,
responsible citizens.'

**What is the Key
Stage 3 National
Strategy?**

'1 ... high expectations
... challenging targets

2 ... strengthening the
transition from KS2

3 ... engage and motivate
... active participation

4 ... strengthening
teaching and learning
through... professional
development'

Section Five: Lessons for the UK – National Educational Initiatives and CSP

The DfES has recently produced the following key papers on national education priorities:

➡ *Delivering Results – A Strategy to 2006*
➡ The Education Bill 2001
➡ *What is the Key Stage 3 National Strategy?*
➡ 14–19 Green Paper: Extending Opportunities, Raising Standards

The aim of this section is to show how the Critical Skills Programme dovetails with each of these initiatives.

1. *Delivering Results – A Strategy to 2006*

The Strategy opens with the following statement:

> 'Our aim is:
>
> To help build a competitive economy and inclusive society by:
>
> ➡ Creating opportunities for everyone to develop their learning.
>
> ➡ Releasing potential in people to make the most of themselves.
>
> ➡ Achieving excellence in standards of education and levels of skills.
>
> 'Our objectives are to:
>
> 1. Give children an excellent start in education so that they have a better foundation for future learning.
> 2. Enable all young people to develop and to equip themselves with the skills, knowledge and personal qualities needed for life and work.
> 3. Encourage and enable adults to learn, improve their skills and enrich their lives.'
>   (*op. cit.* pages 3 and 4)

There is a clear match between these statements and the 'Belief Statement' at the beginning of the *CSP Level 1 Training Manual:*

'We believe that education must be experiential, must nurture interdependence, and must enable all members of each generation to develop the judgement necessary to take responsibility for:

➡ the conduct of their lives,

➡ the shaping of their societies,

➡ and their participation in global issues.

'We believe that judgement is the integration of knowledge, skills and standards of ethical behaviour that guides decisions, commitment and action.'
(*op. cit.* page 4)

Many other clear matches can be made between the CSP model of learning and teaching and the DfES's Strategy document. For example:

DfES Objective 1

This objective concerns the laying of 'a better foundation for future learning.' In CSP, teachers of children as young as five years use the following characteristics which underpin the model:

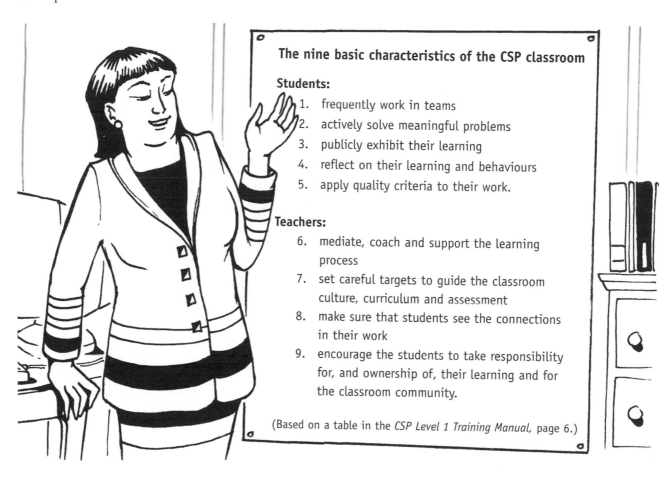

The nine basic characteristics of the CSP classroom

Students:

1. frequently work in teams
2. actively solve meaningful problems
3. publicly exhibit their learning
4. reflect on their learning and behaviours
5. apply quality criteria to their work.

Teachers:

6. mediate, coach and support the learning process
7. set careful targets to guide the classroom culture, curriculum and assessment
8. make sure that students see the connections in their work
9. encourage the students to take responsibility for, and ownership of, their learning and for the classroom community.

(Based on a table in the *CSP Level 1 Training Manual,* page 6.)

All of these characteristics set the foundations for autonomous, life-long learning. In Scotland at the moment, nurseries are using the CSP model with their children, and the youngest children there are three years old! The table overleaf, which is also from the *CSP Level 1 Manual*, shows how carefully designed criteria help teachers to establish these classroom characteristics.

**Students Take Responsibility for and Ownership of their Learning
and for the Classroom Community**

NOVICE

➡ Provides students with choices.

➡ Makes students part of classroom logistics management.

➡ Has students participate in giving peer feedback.

➡ Provides opportunities for student viewpoints.

➡ Engages students in the decision-making process around guidelines for classroom interactions.

➡ Remembers the power of "Who wants the chalk?"

➡ Helps students identify necessary steps of a challenge.

➡ Assigns students roles to help facilitate challenge.

➡ Encourages students to use the teacher as one resource among many (such as peers, books, internet).

INTERMEDIATE

➡ Takes on the role of "resource of last resort."

➡ Provides the opportunity for students to modify challenges to better meet their needs.

➡ Lets students take on most challenge facilitation roles.

➡ Ensures students know the knowledge, skills, and attitudes being targeted in their work.

➡ Leads students to actively reflect on quality.

ADVANCED

Creates an environment where:

➡ Students take the initiative.

➡ Students sometimes help to design and lead challenges.

➡ The teacher is viewed as a member of the collaborative learning community.

➡ Students work effectively without teacher oversight (even when a substitute teacher is there!)

➡ Students are aware, without teacher direction, of the work they need to accomplish.

➡ Students access tools and strategies to help in their problem solving efforts.

➡ Students make arrangements to dedicate time and energy to produce quality work. ·

➡ Students are reflective on the quality of their work and revise to improve quality.

CSP Level 1 Training Manual, page 11

The DfES has set targets for Objective 1, which include increasing the percentage of 11 year olds who achieve Level 4 in each of the Key Stage 2 English and maths tests. Similarly, the advanced CSP practitioner sets learning targets to guide curriculum and assessment using the following criteria:

➡ Develops assessments which connect to knowledge/understanding and skill/behaviour learning standards

➡ Makes knowledge/understanding and skills/behaviours the explicit focus of all student work

➡ Systematically addresses National Curriculum targets with students

➡ Applies learning targets in developing extended classwork

➡ Incorporates students in discussion of the learning targets to be addressed.

(CSP Level 1 Training Manual, page 10)

This constant application of quality criteria to practice in the classroom, and to children's work and behaviour, ensures increasing excellence in standards and in the end products the children produce.

DfES Objective 2

This could have been written by a CSP practitioner. It states:

'The Government is committed to transforming secondary education by improving the quality of teaching and learning for all young people... There will be a focus on improving standards for 11–14-year-olds at Key Stage 3 where progress has too often been too slow.' (*op. cit.* page 8.)

'Working with others we will deliver: ...

➡ A reformed school curriculum incorporating citizenship to support and encourage pupils to become *active citizens and contributors to their communities*.*

➡ Support and encouragement for all schools to develop innovative approaches to raising standards, with new freedom for the most successful secondary schools to lead the way.'* (*op. cit.* page 9 – emphases added)

* Audrey Gibson, Heather Swinson and Jo herself all provide vivid descriptions of the power of the model to transform their students' attitudes and behaviour, (Section 3, vignettes 3, 4 and 10).

* In Section 2 John Kerr describes how the design of challenges is closely linked to curriculum targets, thus helping to raise standards of achievement (pages 35–36).

It would be superfluous to suggest the 'innovative approach' that schools might like to explore in order to raise standards; it speaks for itself!* And with regard to the DfES's 'active citizens and contributors to their communities' the *Level 1 CSP Training Manual* identifies the key attributes of 'responsible and active members of communities' in the following way. Students:

* Pete Fox (Section 3, vignette 1) describes the powerful impact of CSP on the culture and standards of achievement at Gilboa-Conesville Central School.

➡ See themselves as valued members of the community

➡ Draw from an ethical foundation for community relationships

➡ Trust others and are trustworthy within the community

➡ Value, celebrate and tap into diversity among community members

➡ Engage others with respect, honesty, integrity and courtesy

➡ Work to understand and empathise with others

➡ Work to maintain an environment of safety, confidence, mutual esteem and mutual support

➡ Enter into productive group work – helping others to achieve a common goal

➡ Take responsibility for a share of the work – keeping the interest of the community in mind

➡ Share themselves as teachers or mentors of others

➡ Contribute and solicit ideas, opinions and resources

➡ Take an active part in forming and supporting group decisions

➡ Express ideas, feelings and hunches with diplomacy.*

(*op. cit.* page 62)

* See pages 36–43, for a description of how a 'Collaborative classroom learning community' is created.

A 'key attribute' is defined as 'an observable behaviour that provides some evidence of the presence of a skill or attitude in a given individual or group' (*op. cit.* page 47).

* For a complete list of these skills and attitudes, see page 32.

Key attributes have been identified for each of the eight 'critical skills' and seven 'fundamental attitudes' and are thoughtfully and specifically articulated.* This is tremendously helpful for teachers, as it helps us to be very specific about our expectations of the students and allows us to express these expectations very clearly. As the example above illustrates, this is quality material which dovetails neatly with the DfES's targets.

DfES Objective 2 continues:

'There needs to be greater choice at 14, including high-quality vocational and academic opportunities... We need to open debate about the best way to develop a coherent 14–19 phase, which offers all young people real choice and opportunity.' (*op. cit.* page 10)

* 'This is the first time I've not failed.' 'This course makes me feel really valued.' Two sample quotes from Jo's students!

CSP practitioners know that our methodology can offer 14–19 year olds these very things. Underachieving and disaffected students love the approach because it encourages success, often for the first time.* My CSP-trained colleague and I have been able to marry the vocational and key skills elements of our courses for 15–19 year olds so seamlessly that they have failed to notice the English and maths. elements which they have so strenuously resisted in the past! As the *CSP Level 1 Training Manual* puts it:

'CSP is understanding that, in order to develop into independent thinkers and responsible citizens, students need to practice being independent and responsible in the relatively safe environment of school. CSP is recognising that teacher issues, such as how to get kids to learn, are problems that can and should involve the students as well. CSP is believing that in a well-designed learning environment, students and teachers can work together to assure the success of all and, thereby, help develop individuals who contribute to the betterment of the world.' (*op. cit.* page 3)

DfES Objective 3

This seeks to deliver:

'Increased numbers of young people aged 14–19 in schools, colleges and workbased learning, aspiring to progress to higher education.' (*op. cit.* page 11)

It also targets adults lacking literacy and numeracy skills, and those in the workplace:
'...many more people need to be involved in learning, because skills are central to economic success.' (*op. cit.* page 12)

Transforming Teaching & Learning

The importance of the 'critical skills' and 'fundamental attitudes' that people need in order to be successful at work has been emphasised in this book already,* as has the importance of fostering the desire for life-long learning. Adults returning to learn are a different ballgame. They are typically unconfident, ill at ease and insecure. They need to be assured of relevance and work-relatedness. This rarely happens and is responsible for the high non-completion rates so common post-19.

* See, for example, 'How CSP began' on page 32. It is worth emphasising that CSP actually began as an Education Business Partnership project, specifically to address these issues.

In Level 2 training, experienced CSP practitioners are given the following *quality criteria* for 'situated learning' – such as further training for people constructing meaning from new learning in shared social contexts like unemployment:

> ➡ 'Emphasise collaborative work within a consciously structured learning community.
>
> ➡ Students share a sense of place and a common motivational set.*
>
> ➡ Gradually transfer ownership and responsibility to students.
>
> ➡ Design problem-based Challenges* which engage students in authentic contexts – relying on productive collaborative work as the primary tool for the development of community.
>
> ➡ Design into student activities expectations for a variety of products that are created from a range of materials, posing real-world challenges.*
>
> ➡ Use connected learning cycles* to cause students to experience ... exhibit ... reflect – all within the context of interaction with the learning community.'
>
> (*CSP Level 2 Training Manual*, page 9)

* See pages 36–43.

* See pages 44–47.

* See the annotated challenge on page 45.

* See page 168.

Building on both US and UK industries' findings that collaboration and teamwork are key employee skills, the following criteria for 'co-operative/collaborative learning' are also specified in the *Level 2 Manual*:

> ➡ Design problem-based Challenges which engage students in authentic contexts – relying on productive collaborative work as the primary tool for the development of community.
>
> ➡ Design challenges to include specific requirements of both individuals and groups. Use both group and individual reflection, feedback and assessment techniques.*
>
> ➡ Use Scenario Challenges and real-life problems* that cast students in a variety of real-life roles. Use role assignment as a preliminary technique to help students to prepare for identification and assumption of roles on their own.
>
> ➡ Build process expectations into Challenge design. Make consistent use of debriefing, journal-writing and other process/reflection techniques.
>
> ➡ Target specific skills and attitudes within the context of Challenge design.
>
> ➡ Use the collaborative learning community* as foundation for all classroom interactions.
>
> (*op. cit.* page 13)

* See the 'Debrief' subsection on pages 54–57.

* See 'The meaningful context' on pages 49–51.

Again, it has to be said that, given these clearly articulated quality criteria and carefully designed challenges, increased 'teaching excellence' (DfES target no. 4) is guaranteed.

The final section of the Strategy – 'A world-class workforce and modern infrastructure for education and skills' – addresses recruitment and retention of teachers. Much emphasis is placed on their continuing professional development and on leadership programmes for senior management. It can be confidently stated that CSP training, though rigorous and tiring, is also of the highest quality, richly rewarding and almost certainly the best professional development experience that any teacher can undergo! Some typical comments from Level 1 CSP trainees:

2. Education Bill 2001: Summary booklet

➡ **Paragraphs 2.1 and 2.2** of the summary Bill state its mission, as follows:

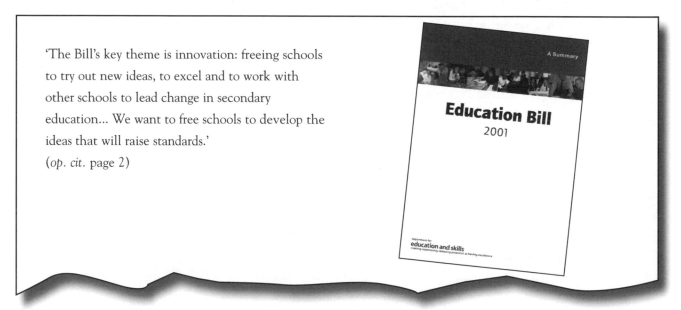

'The Bill's key theme is innovation: freeing schools to try out new ideas, to excel and to work with other schools to lead change in secondary education... We want to free schools to develop the ideas that will raise standards.'

(*op. cit.* page 2)

* See also Theme 2: 'Setting standards for students' work' in Bruce Bonney's article 'Frequently Asked Questions' (page 142–147).

As many of the vignettes in Section 3 make clear, CSP is replete with the kinds of 'ideas that will raise standards' – perhaps even more than the authors of the Bill had thought possible!*

➡ **Paragraph 2.4** goes on to set out some exciting new ideas to encourage this innovation:

'We are therefore introducing a new 'power to innovate'. Where schools or local education authorities have good ideas to raise standards which do not fit the rules as they stand, they will be able to apply to the Secretary of State to vary the legislation as it applies to them for a pilot period. Pilots may last for up to 3 years, with the possibility of extension for up to a further 3 years, with the consent of Parliament. We will seek to learn from these innovative projects and, where they are successful, help other schools to take advantage of them and go back to Parliament to make them permanent (either through further legislation or through a Regulatory Reform Order).' (*op. cit.* page 3)

➡ **Paragraph 2.7** states that barriers which currently prevent schools and colleges from sharing teachers will be removed. From a CSP perspective this is a radical move which will enable those of us who have the requisite training to share expertise locally. It also meshes well with the 'in-house' CSP training packages* which are already proving so popular, as well as the CSP/Network Educational Press ethos that collaboration and community are vital skills and ethical modes of behaviour.

An information pack on these training packages is available from Network Educational Press.

➡ **Paragraph 2.8** talks about the role of schools within their communities:

'Furthermore, schools will be freed to extend the range of services they provide, if they want to, as a resource for the wider community....' (*op. cit.*)

It also encourages schools to work with other service providers. This could open the doors for teachers to design community-based challenges for their students, as is already happening in the USA. It also has implications for the 14–19 flexibility proposals.*

Pete Fox (Section 3, Vignette 1) has created some particularly effective community-based challenges, one of which features in the CSP training video.

➡ **Paragraphs 2.10 – 2.12** outline proposals for the establishment of wholly new schools:

'Where a new secondary school is required ... any promoter, including a community or faith group, an LEA or another public, private or voluntary body can publish proposals' (*op. cit.*)

This, as the Chinese would say, is an interesting innovation. But just imagine establishing a whole school running with the CSP model!*

Gilboa-Conesville Central School (see Pete Fox's vignette, page 66) has been transformed from a 'failing school' into an outstandingly successful one by using the CSP model as a management tool at all levels.

➡ **Paragraphs 3.1 – 3.4** describe how deregulation measures will 'support schools to innovate and develop new ideas' and allow schools to 'work and learn together'. This will be particularly helpful where several schools in the same area are developing the CSP model.*

This is already happening to good effect in various parts of the UK.

→ **Paragraphs 3.5 – 3.9** focus on providing 'new freedoms for the best schools' to allow them to 'vary elements of the National Curriculum' (and) 'create more flexibility in the Key Stage 4 curriculum to allow students to pursue their talents and aspirations...' A core of subjects will remain but there will be greater scope for variation in the rest of the curriculum. There will also be increased opportunity for work-based learning. This is good news as it will allow CSP practitioners to design quality challenges which foster the skills that our young people need to exhibit in the workplace, one of CSP's central themes.

→ Finally, **paragraphs 4.1 – 4.4** outline legislative reform which is basically designed to reduce prescription and constraint on schools which want to introduce innovation but can't at present because the red tape is so prolific and difficult to sever. In summary, then, the words 'flexibility' and 'innovation' appear frequently throughout the Bill, which is good news for those wanting to use CSP to 'transform teaching and learning' in the UK!

3. The Key Stage 3 National Strategy

The Key Stage 3 strategy is based on the following four key principles:

1. expectations

2. progression

3. engagement

4. transformation

Let's examine each of these four principles in turn and compare them to key features of CSP.

1. Expectations – establishing high expectations for all pupils and setting challenging targets for them to achieve

One of the key features of CSP is the idea of high expectations. CSP teachers are trained to design challenges which are stretching and set within tight time-frames. They also set and apply rigorous quality criteria, as shown on page 168.

CSP challenge design is carefully structured, as described in this extract from the *Level 1 Training Manual*:

'The goal of problem-based learning is to create authentic learning experiences for students. As teachers and students first begin to work with problem-based challenges, it is likely that they will be of simple design, and deal with curricular issues only. However, with experience, the emphasis should be on:

→ **increasing authenticity and intellectual rigour for students**
  • forging connections to real-life roles and experiences

- crafting challenges to create real-life contexts through real-life problems

➡ **increasing complexity of the challenges**
- designing multi-dimensional problems that require students to probe, search and connect ideas, information and resources
- building in requirements for higher-order thinking skills such as analysis, synthesis and evaluation

➡ **increasing uncertainty of 'one right answer'**
- designing challenges that move beyond neatly defined and packaged problems with clear-cut answers
- crafting open-ended problems with the potential for several solutions
- creating 'messy' problems that require a high level of problem definition before work on a solution can begin

➡ **increasing variety of resources required for problem-solving**
- crafting challenges that cause students to reach beyond the traditional 'in classroom' or 'in library' reference material – extending their internal definition of resources to include human, primary, technological, community and expert resources

➡ **increasing degrees of student self-direction and self-adjustment**
- working toward full inclusion of students in challenge design, the setting of quality criteria for products and processes, the management of work within challenges and the facilitation of challenge debrief.'
(*op. cit.* pages 72–73 (adapted))

2. Progression – strengthening the transition from Key Stage 2 so that pupils do not fall back in Year 7 and ensuring good progression in teaching and learning across Key Stage 3

In CSP this process is known as 'reflection and connection'. It is absolutely vital if the students are to progress their skills, knowledge and attitudes. It is also an integral part of the experiential learning cycle, as shown below:*

* See also the subsections on self-assessment and peer assessment (pages 55–57), and on transferring skills and connecting knowledge (pages 62–63).

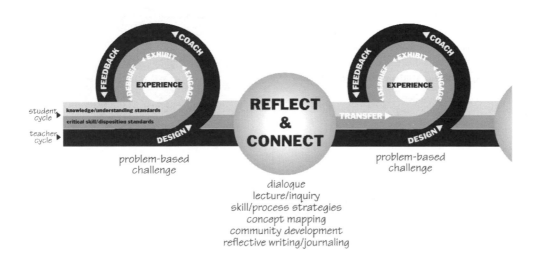

THE EXPERIENTIAL CYCLE PLUS REFLECTION & CONNECTION

© 1997 Critical Skills Program

CSP L1 Coaching Kit

SETTING QUALITY CRITERIA — A PROCEDURE

© 1997 Critical Skills Program

1 **Be clear about the kinds of quality criteria being set:**
   a.   knowledge and understanding: products {see page 68 for examples}
   b.   skills/dispositions {see page 69 for examples}

2 **Determine how quality criteria will be set:**
   a.   established by you
   b.   negotiated with students with your facilitation
   c.   set by students alone

3 **Regardless of how they will be set, create a basic set of quality criteria, even if it will ultimately be for _your_ use only.**

For **_products_** which evidence **_knowledge/understanding_** give consideration to:

► **form criteria**
   What characteristics are essential to quality in the product's form or structure? (example: the poster is large enough to be easily seen from a distance of 10ft.)

► **content criteria**
   What characteristics are essential to quality in the content that the product represents? The focus here is on exhibitions of knowledge and understanding. (example: the poster conveys all the key relationships of the water cycle.)

► **process criteria**
   What characteristics are essential to quality relative to the way in which the product is developed? (example: Is ready for peer review by next Friday.)

► **impact criteria**
   What characteristics are essential to quality relative to the effectiveness of the product in real-world terms? (example: the product does what it is supposed to do!)

For **_skills and dispositions_**, focus on:

► **process criteria**
   What observable behaviors are essential to quality work in a skill or dispositional area? (example: documenting an orderly plan to attack the problem.)

► **impact criteria**
   What observable behaviors are essential to quality relative to effective application of skills/dispositions in real-world terms? (example: arriving at a workable problem solution.)

4 **Present your quality criteria to the students**
   Use a list you've created.

_OR_

Negotiate quality criteria with students
   Give students models of real-world products. Ask them to identify quality characteristics of the product.
   Use language that makes it clear that quality work and processes are the goal that underlies criteria setting.
   Guide students in the brainstorming of criteria.
   Cull, combine, modify criteria — striving for a set that is truly indicative of quality.
   Participate in this process, adding your own criteria as appropriate.

_OR_

Allow students to set their own quality criteria.
   Students can meet with you to "sign-off" on these criteria.

5 **As students engage in work on the challenge, draw their attention back to the criteria.**

   "How does the approach that you are taking here relate to the criteria that have been set?"

   "Does this decision represent a compromise on quality?"

   "Is this quality characteristic working for you? Should we modify it?"

6 **Hold students accountable to their quality criteria.**
   Use the criteria as the basis for assessing student work and giving them feedback.
   Use skill/disposition criteria during debriefing to help students reflect on their processes.

7 **Convert the quality criteria into an assessment rubric.**

8 **Have students self-assess against their quality criteria using the rubric.**

9 **On subsequent challenges, encourage students to improve on their quality criteria.**
   Avoid the pitfall of using criteria as "minimum expectations for a grade."

I seem to have fallen somewhat short of my criterion for vertical.

The 'reflection and connection' process allows the teacher to address such issues as:

➡ 'What are the key concepts of the work we've been doing? Do we have command of those concepts? How do they interconnect? Is there something more we need to explore at this point to enhance our understanding?

➡ How does what we learned in this challenge connect to other work we have done or to other things we understand? How does this work and its key concepts connect to other, bigger ideas? Why is this work important?

➡ Are there particular skills that need our attention or are there skills strategies that would benefit us now? What do we need to do to tackle the next challenge more effectively?

➡ How well are we working together as a learning community? Is there a need for community-building or maintenance, or for conflict resolution?'

(*CSP Level 1 Training Manual*, page 152)

The table below gives reasons for all of these questions and provides a 'toolkit' of methods for addressing them.

REFLECTION & CONNECTION — WHAT, WHY, HOW

© 1997 Critical Skills Program

What?	Why?	How?
Connecting to past and future content/concepts	▶ to identify/highlight/reinforce key concepts ▶ to show the importance and relevance of the experience ▶ to clear up misconceptions and identify understanding gaps ▶ to help students to make the vital connections among experiences that result in true understanding	* carousel/distillation (page 160) * WASH (page 158-159) * discussion * reflection on key questions/themes * graphic organizers (page 157) * test/quiz
"Un"covering new material	▶ to teach and/or clarify concepts and share information students need to know ▶ to connect ideas from the challenge to related ideas ▶ to meet the needs of those who benefit from direct presentation of concepts	* lecture * discussion * videos * mini-challenge * research
Focusing on skill development	▶ to develop understanding of the key attributes of skills, that is, what skills look like/sound like/feel like when well done ▶ to prepare students for work on subsequent challenges	* brainstorm characteristics of important skills * standard operating procedure (page 162-163) * role playing of skill use * skits
Community development and maintenance	▶ to develop and maintain a classroom culture that results in a community of learners prepared to support and enhance the learning of all its members ▶ to develop attitude of safety and fairness among group members: point out successes and problems and address them ▶ to maintain focus on quality work; to acknowledge success and problems	* check-in — how are we doing? * feed-back - how I think you are doing * games/initiatives (page 36-42) * revisit/develop FVC (page 29-32) * IP3 debriefing/planning (page 161) * community meeting (page 35)
Working on collaborative process/problems	▶ to move group forward toward greater efficiency in future collaborative work ▶ to foster ownership of collaborative processes	* standard operating procedure (page 162-163) * discussion * mediation

CSP L1 Training Manual

In Level 2 Training, CSP practitioners learn the complex art of designing a sequence of related learning experiences, and how to help students to make connections to previous work and to their worlds outside school. As the *Level 2 Training Manual* puts it:

'A developing CSP expert ...

➡ Uses the experiential learning cycle to revisit learning standards (curriculum targets) in a range of experiences.

➡ Builds on previous challenges to broaden, deepen, and enhance understanding.

➡ Looks for opportunities to connect and expand on key concepts and big ideas.

➡ Frames experiences with essential questions.

➡ Uses observation and assessment of previous work as the basis for future work. Adjusts as necessary.

➡ Makes teaching connections to children's lives outside school.

➡ Builds on previous challenge experiences to increase the complexity and authenticity of the work.'

(*op. cit.* page 152)

3. Engagement – promoting approaches to teaching and learning that engage and motivate pupils and demand their active participation

* See also 'The Pupil Cycle' (pages 51–57).

This of course is what CSP problem-based challenges are all about.* Here, for example, is what the *Level 1 Training Manual* says about them:

'Problem-based learning is a primary feature of a CSP classroom. Problem-based learning is the use of carefully crafted and connected challenges as the primary (but not exclusive!) teaching vehicle. These challenges pose a problem for students to solve, as individuals, in small groups, or as a full learning community.

'Why problem-based learning? Because it is the most effective way we know to turn responsibility for learning over to students. Students have to think and act for themselves in order to solve a problem. They simply cannot remain passive. They must interact with information, people, resources, situations, and tools. Through problem-based learning, students gain vital experience with problem-solving – a dominant feature of all our daily lives.

'In a CSP classroom, students are given opportunities to engage in both small and large challenges – problems that span a few minutes to a few weeks. Problem-based learning is a powerful methodology. However, it is important to remember that no single methodology addresses all student needs. In between problems, a wide variety of teaching approaches are used to enhance and reinforce student understanding.' (*op. cit.* page 17)

4. Transformation – strengthening teaching and learning through a programme of professional development and practical support

Almost all of the several hundred UK teachers who have already taken CSP training would undoubtedly agree that it is a 'programme of professional development and practical support' of the highest quality. Indeed, I would argue that, since it meshes so completely with all four of these key principles, CSP is the obvious way forward for Key Stage 3 practitioners.

As professionals, we spend an inordinate amount of time behind closed doors re-inventing the pedagogical wheel. Why do this, when there's material of this quality available, written and refined over many years by experienced, practising teachers?

In a speech titled 'Transforming Secondary Education' (21 March 2002) Secretary of State for Education Estelle Morris talked of the challenges facing middle years schooling around the world (para.19). Describing various approaches in other countries, she observed that 'No one can yet claim to have found the golden key.' OK, nothing is absolutely perfect, but CSP is pretty close. It's at least the silver key!* The Critical Skills Programme has already transformed my classroom, and those of hundreds of other teachers in this country alone. It is the way forward for transformation.

* Or as primary teacher Joyce Kirkland put it: 'I did not think I would see the Holy Grail in my lifetime in teaching. But I think Critical Skills could be it.'

4. 14–19 Green Paper: Extending Opportunities, Raising Standards: Summary document

The introduction to this document contains the following interesting observation:

'The pace of economic change has not been matched by the pace of change in our education system' (*op. cit.* page 2)

14–19:
extending opportunities, raising standards
Summary

education and skills

The following analogy sums the situation up neatly. If you were a nineteenth-century surgeon transplanted into a modern-day operating theatre, the most you'd be able to contribute would be to mop the odd brow. However, if you were a nineteenth-century teacher and were transported to a typical, modern-day classroom, the odds are that you'd know where you were immediately and start to teach. That cannot be right in the twenty-first century.

The introduction also states:

'Young people must be prepared for an adult life in which they are involved as active, responsible citizens... For young people themselves the price of disengagement from learning is often serious problems and persistent failure for the rest of their lives.' (*op. cit.* page 1)

I don't need to say what I believe is the obvious solution...! However, let's examine some meeting points between the Green Paper and CSP.

➡ **The vision** of the paper is that 14–19 education should:

- 'meet the needs and aspirations of all young people ...;
- raise the levels of achievement of all young people ...;
- broaden the skills acquired by all young people ...;*
- be delivered through flexible, integrated and innovative networks of providers ...'

➡ **The proposals** for achieving this vision can be summarised as:

- 'a more flexible (post-14) curriculum ...;
- 'world class' technical and vocational education ...;
- a Matriculation Diploma at 19;
- pastoral support and guidance;
- inclusivity for all 14–19-year-olds, regardless of ethnicity, income or ability;
- closer collaboration between providers;
- more effective use of ICT and e-learning.'

➡ **the outcomes** sought from the 14–19 phase are:

- 'higher levels of participation and ... attainment;
- a commitment to lifelong learning ...;
- increased employability ...;
- more rounded, more motivated and more responsible citizens ...;
- a reduction in ... truanting and ... dropping out ...;
- a greatly improved 14–19 system of education ...'

The Green Paper suggests a progress review at age 14, with individual action planning.* The curriculum would include core subjects; learning for personal development; and wider activities in the community. The Matriculation Diploma would recognise all three of these strands. GCSE and its equivalents would mark a progress check around the midpoint of the phase.

➡ English, maths, science and ICT will be mandatory, along with citizenship, RE, careers, sex and health education, PE and work-related learning. In addition, all students are to access a foreign language, design and technology, the arts and humanities. Given the additional curricular flexibility, disapplication of some requirements of the National Curriculum will no longer apply, except for statemented students.

➡ Work-related programmes will be extended for the full spectrum of students, with clear vocational routes to higher education. There will be more vocational qualifications, and all GCSEs will be indentified by subject title only, in order to remove the current distinction between 'academic' and 'vocational' subjects.

➡ More demanding questions will be introduced into A2 papers in order to allow differentiation for those students able to demonstrate knowledge, skills and understanding gained through wider study – either vocationally, academically or

Transforming Teaching & Learning

through working in the wider community. Separate labelling of general and vocational A levels may be dropped once the structure of vocational A levels is aligned with the present model of AS/A2.

➡ The Matriculation Diploma should motivate more students to subscribe to education to age 19. The Green Paper holds that it will widen horizons and point the way towards greater coherence within programmes young people choose to pursue. It will promote parity between vocational and academic subjects; encourage the development of the 'whole person'; and discourage narrow programmes of study. It will be awarded at three levels:

Intermediate - for those achieving at Level 2 (equivalent to 5+ GCSEs at A*-C; intermediate GNVQ or NVQ2);

Advanced – for Level 3 (equivalent to 2+ A levels, Advanced GNVQ or NVQ3); and

Higher – based on broader achievement than Advanced.

The diploma will also allow for pace, in that some young people need more time than others to achieve. A Matriculation Certificate may be provided in acknowledgement of other achievements, undifferentiated by level.

Interestingly, the Green Paper also addresses 'pace and progression'.* It proposes that some students may take GCSEs earlier, or bypass them entirely to progress to AS. 'When ready' tests are being developed which can be taken on-line. GCSEs may also be taken post-16.

* See the passage on 'progression' on pages 168–70.

These proposals imply the need for greater guidance and support for young people, so the Connexions Service is being established to provide just that. Connexions Service Personal Advisers will monitor and review action plans to ensure wise choice post-16, and to make sure that the requirements of the Matriculation Diploma are being met. They will also broker flexible vocational/academic programmes and encourage wider community involvement.

Financial support will be available to 16–19-year-old students, to encourage them to stay on in learning. A Connexions Card will give them discounts on study-related costs and there will be incentives for attendance and application. Access funds will continue to be available.

All of these reforms are planned to be in place fully by 2005–06, while 'pathfinder projects' will be running from 2002–03.

Clearly, it would be unnecessary duplication to match the aims and methodology of CSP against these proposals. The implications should by now be clear. In particular, other CSP practitioners* have described the fundamental changes in attitudes of young people exposed to CSP methodology.

* See, for example, Vignettes 3, 4 and 10 in Section 3.

Regardless of context, those of us involved in change – (and for UK educators continuous, significant change has been going on for far too long a time) – undergo predictable and necessary stages of development and adaptation. These are illustrated in the table overleaf which is taken from the *CSP Level 1 Training Manual*. The significant educational initiatives described in this section will open a new phase of change, but this time – with the help of CSP – it may well be for the better.

	Novice ▶	Apprentice ▶	Practitioner ▶	Expert ▶	Leader
Behavioral	experimentation	implementation		adaptation	innovation
Affective	emergence	ownership		integration	judgment
Social	dependence	independence		interdependence	mentoring
Cognitive	revelation	focus		connection	internalization
	algorithm dependence		prototype recognition		pattern making

CSP L1 Coaching Kit

CSP practitioners throughout the UK will undoubtedly respond to many of these proposals with delight, and could spearhead the innovation and internalisation that the Government is advocating. As Gandhi said, 'if change is to happen, it starts with me.' Individuals can make a difference. Each of us has a vested interest in the greatest good for the greatest number of students in our care. As the old adage has it:

Teachers affect eternity— who knows where our influence ends?

Those of us who have experienced the power of CSP now have the opportunity to demonstrate its relevance to the targets set out in these Government initiatives. Let's seize this opportunity to bring to the Government's attention, in whatever ways we can, that CSP is the way forward for education in the twenty-first century. As one senior educationalist (Di Buck of Success@EAZ, Bristol) commented after experiencing Level 1 CSP training:

I feel sure that CSP is the way forward for us and for our children. This must be central to the thinking of all in education!

Bibliography

Black, P. and Wiliam, D. (1998) *Inside the Black Box: Raising Standards Through Classroom Assessment*. King's College London School of Education.

Department for Education and Skills (2002) *What is the Key Stage 3 National Strategy?* www.standards.dfes.gov.uk/keystage3/about_ks3

Department for Education and Skills (2001) *The Education Bill 2001*. HMSO.

Department for Education and Skills (2002) *Delivering Results: A Strategy to 2006*. HMSO.

Department for Education and Skills (2002) *14–19 Green Paper: Extending Opportunities, Raising Standards*. HMSO.

Gardner, H. (1993) *Frames of Mind: The Theory of Multiple Intelligences* (second edition). Fontana.

Grisham, D. and Molinelli, P. (1995) *Co-operative Learning*. Teacher Created Materials, Inc.

Hay McBer (2000) *Research into Teacher Effectiveness*. DfEE.

Heathcote, D. (1984) 'Signs and Portents' in *Collected Writings on Education and Drama*. Hutchinson.

HM Inspectors of Schools (Scotland) Quality Standards and Audit Unit (1996) *How Good is our School? Self-evaluation Using Performance Indicators*. HMSO.

Mobilia, W. et. al. (1999) *The Critical Skills Programme Level 2 Training Manual*. Antioch New England Graduate School/Network Educational Press.

Mobilia, W. et. al. (2000) *The Critical Skills Programme Level 1 Training Manual*. Antioch New England Graduate School/Network Educational Press.

Postman, N. and Weingartner, C. (1969) *Teaching as a Subversive Activity*. Penguin.

Weatherley, C. (2000) *Leading the Learning School*. Network Educational Press.

Index

N

National Curriculum 166
- targets 160
New England 67, 121
'New Start' 109, 110
New York State 11, 66, 67, 111, 121
NVQ 173

O

observation checklist 104
OfSTED 94, 95, 116
'old fashioned teaching' 74
'on task' 73, 90
open-ended tasks 55, 59
opportunities 158
organisation 146
organisational chaos 97
organisational culture 123
outcomes 36, 45, 47, 140
ownership 77, 95, 99, 100, 140, 159, 160, 163

P

panel presentations 107, 126, 137, 153
parents 66, 73, 75, 124, 126, 134, 149
pedagogical debate 107
peer assessment 57, 61, 74, 93, 108, 116
'people' people 48
performance indicators 104, 124, 147
performance management 96
Personal and Social Development 104
personalities 38, 47–48, 99, 104, 140, 141, 151
'picture on the lid of the jigsaw' 92
'Plan of the Day' 83
planning 100
potential 158
poverty 66
practice 143
praise 94, 138
presentation 86, 90, 98, 100, 107, 117, 126
problem-based learning 33, 44, 69, 144, 170
problem solving 76–77, 79, 106, 137, 146, 159
process 77
process classroom 69
process criteria 60, 142–143
'process' people 48
product(s) 90, 124, 147
product criteria 74, 142–143
'product' people 48
product quality checklist 61–62
professional development 94, 96, 133, 164, 170
professional judgement 124

professionally mature 131, 132
professional scepticism 131
progression 73, 168–170, 173
public performance 126
pupil cycle 34, 51–57
pupil ownership 77

Q

quality discussion 84, 150
- standards 37, 38, 106, 134, 143
quality audience 40, 84, 90, 104, 144, 150, 152, 153
- standards 37, 106
quality criteria 54, 79, 134, 140, 142–143, 144, 159, 161, 163
quality feedback 135–136

R

ranking 108
R E 92, 93, 95
real-life challenge 46, 51, 84, 114
recorders 79, 85, 143
recruitment of teachers 164
reflection 54, 56, 89, 90, 91, 94, 96, 98, 100, 112, 122, 133, 134, 135, 146, 159
- and connection 63, 81, 152, 159, 163, 168–170
reinforcement 89
'repair kit' 117
resources 78, 79, 107, 165, 167
respect 68, 98, 107
respected 131
responsibility 140, 152, 159, 160, 163, 170, 171
results-driven learning 33
review 54, 89, 112
revitalised 75, 105
'right brain' 53
risk taking 69, 129, 137
'road to Damascus' 93
rubric 104, 152
rule criteria 54, 61, 77–78, 79

S

'sage on the stage' 74
sarcasm 150–151
SATs 105
scenario challenge 46, 50–51, 74, 107, 108
scepticism 132, 149
school failure 66
school management 104
school monitoring and evaluation 96
'Schoolopoly' 84
self-assessment 55–56, 74, 108, 112

Other Publications

THE SCHOOL EFFECTIVENESS SERIES

Book 1: *Accelerated Learning in the Classroom* by Alistair Smith
ISBN: 185539-034-5

Book 2: *Effective Learning Activities* by Chris Dickinson
ISBN: 185539-035-3

Book 3: *Effective Heads of Department* by Phil Jones & Nick Sparks
ISBN: 185539-036-1

Book 4: *Lessons are for Learning* by Mike Hughes
ISBN: 185539-038-8

Book 5: *Effective Learning in Science* by Paul Denley and Keith Bishop
ISBN: 185539-039-6

Book 6: *Raising Boys' Achievement* by Jon Pickering
ISBN: 185539-040-X

Book 7: *Effective Provision for Able & Talented Children* by Barry Teare
ISBN: 1-85539-041-8

Book 8: *Effective Careers Education & Guidance* by Andrew Edwards and Anthony Barnes
ISBN: 1-85539-045-0

Book 9: *Best behaviour and Best behaviour FIRST AID* by
Peter Relf, Rod Hirst, Jan Richardson and Georgina Youdell
ISBN: 1-85539-046-9

Best behaviour FIRST AID
ISBN: 1-85539-047-7   (pack of 5 booklets)

Book 10: *The Effective School Governor* by David Marriott
ISBN 1-85539-042-6   (including free audio tape)

Book 11: *Improving Personal Effectiveness for Managers in Schools* by James Johnson
ISBN 1-85539-049-3

Book 12: *Making Pupil Data Powerful* by Maggie Pringle and Tony Cobb
ISBN 1-85539-052-3

Book 13: *Closing the Learning Gap* by Mike Hughes
ISBN 1-85539-051-5

Book 14: *Getting Started* by Henry Leibling
ISBN 1-85539-054-X

Book 15: *Leading the Learning School* by Colin Weatherley
ISBN 1-85539-070-1

Book 16: *Adventures in Learning* by Mike Tilling
ISBN 1-85539-073-6

Book 17: *Strategies for Closing the Learning Gap* by Mike Hughes & Andy Vass
ISBN 1-85539-075-2

Book 18: *Classroom Management* by Phillip Waterhouse and Chris Dickinson
ISBN 1-85539-079-5

Book 19: *Effective Teachers* by Tony Swainston
ISBN 1-85539-125-2

ACCELERATED LEARNING SERIES

General Editor: **Alistair Smith**

Accelerated Learning in Practice by Alistair Smith
ISBN 1-85539-048-5

The ALPS Approach: Accelerated Learning in Primary Schools
by Alistair Smith and Nicola Call
ISBN 1-85539-056-6

MapWise by Oliver Caviglioli and Ian Harris
ISBN 1-85539-059-0

The ALPS Approach Resource Book by Alistair Smith and Nicola Call
ISBN 1-85539-078-7

Creating an Accelerated Learning School by Mark Lovatt & Derek Wise
ISBN 1-85539-074-4

ALPS StoryMaker by Stephen Bowkett
ISBN 1-85539-076-0

Thinking for Learning by Mel Rockett & Simon Percival
ISBN 1-85539-096-5

Reaching out to all learners by Cheshire LEA
ISBN 1-85539-143-0

EDUCATION PERSONNEL MANAGEMENT SERIES

These new Education Personnel Management handbooks will help headteachers, senior managers and governors to manage a broad range of personnel issues.

The Well Teacher – management strategies for beating stress, promoting staff health and reducing absence by Maureen Cooper
ISBN 1-85539-058-2

Managing Challenging People – dealing with staff conduct by Bev Curtis and Maureen Cooper
ISBN 1-85539-057-4

Managing Poor Performance – handling staff capability issues
by Bev Curtis and Maureen Cooper
ISBN 1-85539-062-0

Managing Allegations Against Staff – personnel and child protection issues in schools
by Maureen Cooper
ISBN 1-85539-072-8

VISIONS OF EDUCATION SERIES

The Unfinished Revolution by John Abbott and Terry Ryan
ISBN 1-85539-064-7

The Learning Revolution by Jeannette Vos & Gordon Dryden
ISBN 1-85539-085-X

Wise Up by Guy Claxton
ISBN 1-85539-099-X

ABLE & TALENTED CHILDREN COLLECTION

Effective Resources for Able and Talented Children by Barry Teare
ISBN 1-85539-050-7

More Effective Resources for Able and Talented Children by Barry Teare
ISBN 1-85539-063-9

Challenging Resources for Able and Talented Children by Barry Teare
ISBN 1-85539-122-8

MODEL LEARNING

Thinking Skill & Eye Q by Oliver Caviglioli, Ian Harris & Bill Tindall
ISBN 1-85539-091-4

Class Maps by Oliver Caviglioli & Ian Harris
ISBN 1-85539-139-2

OTHER TITLES FROM NEP

The Brain's Behind It by Alistair Smith
ISBN 1-85539-083-3

Help Your Child To Succeed by Bill Lucas & Alistair Smith
ISBN 1-85539-111-2

Becoming Emotionally Intelligent by Cath Corrie
ISBN 1-85539-069-8

Tweak to Transform by Mike Hughes
ISBN 1-85539-140-6

Brain Friendly Revision by UFA National Team
ISBN 1-85539-127-9

Numeracy Activities Key Stage 2 by Afzal Ahmed & Honor Williams
ISBN 1-85539-102-3

Numeracy Activities Key Stage 3 by Afzal Ahmed, Honor Williams & George Wickham
ISBN 1-85539-103-1

Imagine That... by Stephen Bowkett
ISBN 1-85539-043-4

Self-Intelligence by Stephen Bowkett
ISBN 1-85539-055-8

Class Talk by Rosemary Sage
ISBN 1-85539-061-2